Responsa From The Holocaust

Translated from Sheilos Utshuvos Mima'makim

By **Rabbi Ephraim Oshry**

Translated by Y. Leiman

Judaica Press • 1983
New York

Distributed By:
Israel Book Shop, Inc.
410 Harvard St.
Brookline, Mass. 02146

MANUFACTURED IN THE UNITED STATES OF AMERICA

Printed by Moriah Offset

Contents

Introduction vii
Foreword xii
Lithuania and Its Jews xv

1941
Outrage
Begins

1. *Endangering Yourself to Save Another* 1
2. *A Kohein Who Was Forced to Convert* 3
3. *Shaving with a Razor* 5
4. *Making a Tahara in Advance* 7
5. *Jews Forced to Shred a Torah Scroll* 9
6. *Sabbath Torah Reading for Slave Laborers* 11
7. *Cooking on the Sabbath in the Ghetto* 13
8. *May a Person Save Himself by Causing
   the Death of a Fellow Jew?* 14
9. *Using the Garments of Martyred Jews* 17
10. *Blowing a Cracked Shofar* 19
11. *Bringing Tefilin into a Hospital Where
    All Personal Objects Are Burned* 20
12. *Eventual Danger to Life* 22
13. *Critically Ill Patients Fasting on Yom Kipur* 23
14. *Sanctioning Unsatisfactory Religious Marriages* 25
15. *A Suka of Boards Stolen from the Germans* 28
16. *Pre-Dawn Donning of Tefilin and Praying* 30
17. *Making up Lost Prayers* 32
18. *Commiting Suicide to Be Buried Among Jews* 34
19. *The Blessing for Martyrdom* 36
20. *Taking the Property of the Dead* 38
21. *Reusing the Garments of Martyrs* 39
22. *Reciting the HaGomel Blessing* 40
23. *Saying Kaddish for Martyrs* 42
24. *Circumcision by an Irreligious Jew* 44

1942 to 1944
Holocaust

25. *Reading of Shema by Slave Laborers* 49
26. *Electric Lights as Shaboss Candles* 50
27. *Eating Soaked Matza to Fulfill the Passover Mitzva* 51
28. *Unsalted Meat and Bloody Carrion* 54
29. *Redeeming a Firstborn Son on Behalf of the Father* 56
30. *Learning Torah with Nazi Murderers* 58
31. *Fulfilling the Mitzva of a Purim Meal with Soup* 60
32. *The Crushed Kohein* 62
33. *Saving Oneself with a Baptismal Certificate* 64
34. *Chametz that Cannot Be Sold Before Passover* 65
35. *Fulfilling the Mitzva of the Four Cups on Passover in the Ghetto* 67
36. *Passover in the Ghetto* 69
37. *Contraceptives in the Ghetto* 71
38. *Performing a Caesarean Section on a Dead Woman* 72
39. *A Man the Germans Beat Deaf and Dumb* 74
40. *Reciting Nacheim in Grace After the Meal on Tisha BeAv* 76
41. *Risking One's Life to Study Torah or to Pray* 78
42. *Abortion in the Ghetto* 81
43. *A Castrated Man as a Cantor* 82
44. *Cremation to Avoid Burial Among Gentiles* 83
45. *Reciting "Who has not made me a slave,"* 85
46. *Opening a Grave to Remove Lost Property* 86
47. *Eating in the Presence of a Corpse* 88
48. *Kohanim Wearing Shoes While Blessing the People* 89
49. *Chametz After Passover* 91
50. *Public Prayer with Hidden Participants* 93
51. *Does a Ghetto Home Need a Mezuza?* 95
52. *Tzitzis Made from Stolen German Wool* 97
53. *Burying a Sabbath Desecrator Among Observers* 99
54. *A Man Whose Left Hand the Germans Amputated* 101
55. *The Hoarse Kohein* 103
56. *Risking One's Life to Join the Partisans* 105
57. *Praying on Tisha BeAv Morning with Talis and Tefilin* 108

58. *May a Jew write the Letters R.C.*
    (Roman Catholic) in His Passport? 110
59. *Greeting Fellow-Jews Bareheaded* 111
60. *Donning Tefilin before Bar Mitzva* 113
61. *The Right to Risk One's Life* 116
62. *Taking a Lulav on the Sabbath* 120
63. *Entrusting Jewish Children to Non-Jews* 123
64. *Reciting Kaddish for Infants* 125

1944 to Present
Horrors unto the Third Generation

65. *Entering a Church* 129
66. *May Circumcision Follow Redemption of the Firstborn?* 131
67. *Mohel and Doctor in Conflict over Circumcision* 133
68. *Anesthesia for Circumcision* 136
69. *Fulfilling One's Obligation for Shema by Hearing It* 138
70. *Bar-Mitzva or Not?* 140
71. *Self-Redemption of a Firstborn Son* 141
72. *A Father's Name for an Adopted Child* 142
73. *The Son Named After His Presumably Dead Father* 144
74. *Circumcising on Shaboss a Child Born to a Jewish*
    Mother from a Gentile Father 146
75. *Seeking Out the Murderers of One's Parents* 148
76. *Reciting Mi Shebeirach for a Gentile* 150
77. *Burying the Bones of Martyrs* 151
78. *Transferring Martyrs' from a Non-Jewish Cemetery* 153
79. *Using Gold from the Teeth of the Dead* 155
80. *Reinterring a Jewess Buried Among Gentiles* 156
81. *Using a Gravestone with a Cross* 157
82. *A Tombstone that Does not Mark a Grave* 158
83. *Using Trees from a Cemetery* 160
84. *A Sidewalk Paved with Jewish Gravestones* 162
85. *Reciting Kaddish for a Gentile Woman* 164
86. *Burying the Remains of Torah Arks* 166

87. *An Ark Curtain Used by a Non-Jew* 168
88. *Utilizing the Cover of a Torah-Scroll* 169
89. *What to Do with Fragments of a Torah-Scroll* 171
90. *The Sunken Torah Scroll* 173
91. *Erasing Transferred Torah Script* 175
92. *Torah Scrolls, Tefilin, and Mezuzos Found*
    in the Possession of Non-Jews 177
93. *Torah Volumes Abused by Gentiles* 178
94. *Returning Sacred Works to Their Owners* 180
95. *Using a Paroches for a Chupa* 182
96. *The Child of a Jewish Woman and a Non-Jew* 183
97. *A Married Woman Who Bore a Gentile's Child* 187
98. *The Case of the Mamzer Rabbi* 190
99. *Women Prostituted by the Germans* 193
100. *Removing Numbers Branded by the Germans*
     on Their Victims 195
101. *The Cross on The Biceps* 197
102. *People Who Lived as Gentiles and Are Now*
     Returning to the Jewish Fold 198
103. *May One Who Disguised Himself As a Catholic*
     Correct Torah Scrolls? 199
104. *A Jew Who Defended Murderers of Jews* 201
105. *Penance for Owning a Passport Identifying*
     Oneself as a Catholic 204
106. *The Repentant Kapo* 206
107. *A Kapo's Name* 207
108. *A Kohein Who Converted to Christianity* 208
109. *Burying a Possible Apostate* 210
110. *May a Mercy Killer Lead Prayers?* 212
111. *A Kohein Who Killed A Gentile* 215
112. *Cannibalism* 218

Introduction

THE WORLD THAT ONCE WAS no longer is. Gone are the holy
communities, the sainted Jews, the children and their
mothers, the rabbis, the libraries of thousands of sacred
books adding up to hundreds of millions, the holy Torah-
scrolls and Friday-night candlesticks and Saturday-night
spice boxes. A world that no historian, sociologist,
anthropologist, writer will ever be able to reconstruct — not
even a hair of it, a shadow.

A thousand years of life in Europe spanning the entire
continent — gone. Disappeared. Destroyed. Read the books,
the yearly announcements of survivors' gatherings, the
exhibits put together by different cultural organizations
whose members have crawled back into the cold gas
chambers to bring back memories, men who have returned
to the towns and cities of their births to bring back
mementos — pieces of the past. Part of a door, a snapshot of a
street in 1939, anything, so long as one can say, "I am
connected, I am part of this destroyed world."

Ironically, what some people retrieve demonstrates the
completeness of the destruction. One man finds a folio of the
Talmud that didn't burn completely and puts it behind a
glass case next to a Jewish Polish hat that was worn by a
young man who more than likely perished in Treblinka.

In passing, I express my loathing for those who were never
there but have "returned" to seek personal advancement or
money; the late poet, Dovid Zaritsky, expressed his anguish
at this development as early as 1947 in his poem, *To the
Mourners:*

> ...and because I have seen that you are being drowned in the
> tears of the mourners

who repeatedly bury and bedeck and be*kaddish* your
memory...
they constantly shoulder ready sacks of tears...
and a pen — filled with Jewish blood — in one hand!
And they have pretty tears, polished, they cry beautifully...
When the sack of tears is opened the whole world gets wet!
If the pen dries up, it is refilled with Jewish blood...
and every so often the wound is torn open, when a word
is needed for a rhyme — it must be had — every word is paid
for
Gold pieces spill from the eyes into the pockets...

*

Seven long years our nation breathes in constant anguish.
Now he stands with bloody, painful bits-of-soul and lung!
And millions of wild hands and tens of millions of clubs
day and night joyfully pummel his aged head...
So what is needed, eh? What do we need, I ask you, providers!
Your minds, your Jewish hearts are needed, not your
mourning tongues,
a mind to find the word that a mother would use for an only
son,
to suddenly push years of anguish aside and shake
despondency from her shoulders.
A mind that is filled with sacred thoughts about the nation —
and has no room for diluted tears produced by a typewriter —
will have such a word!

Translated by Hiyela Housman. Copyright 1980 by Light
Magazine, Inc. Used with permission.

What does it mean when what we've retrieved from the
past are sentimental curiosities which are nothing more
than anthropological artifacts — fodder for the Jewish
nostalgianiks whose relationship to Judaism is measured in
terms of glass cases in a museum?

This book exists partly because I also wanted to save something from that world. The story is simple. The war came and the ghettoes were created. I was a young rabbi in the Kovno of Lithuania whose greats were known throughout the Jewish world.

People, the plain people, approached me with their questions. Because life was not normal and there was a war on, they were not always sure what the Torah required of them. Source books were not available, and I could not rule on these questions the way I would have in normal times. My memory had to serve me. But I did note down the questions and my brief rulings on paper torn from cement sacks which I hid in cans that I buried in the ghetto soil to preserve them. If I survived, I'd expand the notes into full-length responses.

I felt that I was not simply burying a diary for the sake of preserving a historical record — although that would have been sufficient. The daily life of the ghetto, the food we ate, the crowded quarters we shared, the rags on our feet, the lice in our skin, the relationships between men and women, the attitudes of German officers — all this was contained within the specifics of the questions; these are the memories they arouse.

How did a 1942 Jew, hauled off under the whip of the German beast, retain a sense of chosenness? How could he feel part of G-d's anointed people, while he watched with his own eyes the denigration of the elders of a generation, the saints and the scholars? For one of the first actions performed by the sons of the government bankers and the illiterate farmers marching side by side for the glory of Germany upon entering a town was to grab any Jew with a beard, the age-old symbol of the Jew, and to remove it.

For the Germans, this torture provided perverse pleasure. No elaborate techniques were needed, no wooden contraptions, no water hoses, not even razor blades. All a soldier had to do was stick his hand into a Jewish beard and pull. What did he care if a layer of skin came out with a handful of hair? Pain? Good! Let that remind the Jew that the beard is foul and disgusting and he has no right to wear one in the first place. It offends German eyes nurtured on the beauty of landscapes, on feminine pulchritude, and on the bottoms of beer steins.

The rabbis ruled that the Jews, in this instance, must shave their beards. Yet two Jews in Kovno didn't, the Chief Rabbi himself and a *chassid* of Chabad. Everyone else complied. Walking through the streets and seeing the faces of these Jews without their beards was like seeing them suddenly naked. One had to avert one's eyes. The shock of seeing the holy faces, some with bloody bandages hiding the scars of recent attacks, and others simply stripped of their glory, was like a knife wound in our souls.

This savage swipe at the Jewish face, like a tiger clawing at its prey, was enough for us to begin to walk with our heads bowed, ashamed before the enemy who had robbed us of our physical distinctiveness.

We wondered, "Is this the end of our exile, or the beginning of some greater destruction? Is it possible that civilized Germany, the purveyor of culture and art and science, has nothing better to do with its lust than to strike at Jewish beards!"

When we realized that we were the targets of the Germans just because we were Jews — that our Jewishness was being attacked — then our Jewish pride came to the fore.

Jews whose faith was strong faced the events that developed with the vigor of the believer. I am not speaking of wonderworking rabbis or of grocers who secretly and humbly had mastered the Talmud and Kabala, but simple Jews whose faith in the Almighty was the core of their being. Such a Jew simply follows the dictates of the Torah as he knows best. And when he doesn't know, he approaches a rabbi, whose authority and wider knowledge and accessiblity to sources is recognized and relied upon.

And so, Jews approaced me. Through the divine watchfulness of G-d, I survived and was able to return and forage for the cans of questions and answers I had hidden away.

Right after the war I dug up my notes on the questions and my answers, and proceeded to examine the sources at greater length and fill out the answers. Only then did I begin to perceive the significance of these questions as a record of Jewish uniqueness. And I was awed by the privilege granted me by Providence to be the scribe who recorded these questions asked in the depths and the responses that emerged from the depths of misery and degradation, of suffering and death, and of resurrection.

Did our enemies, the Germans — many of them churchgoing sons of churchgoing mothers and fathers — ask their priests and ministers how to care for the Jewish dead? Were they concerned to learn whether one may use clothes stolen from a dead Jew, or a curtain ripped from the ark where the Torah-scrolls are kept? Did they receive dispensation to bayonet pregnant mothers?

But we Jews did inquired as to the proper prayers to say after food when forced to eat on a fast day. We wanted to know the correct form of the blessing a Jew says before going to his death in sanctification of G-d.

The world at large may not understand this. But the greatness of the Jew can be seen in these very concerns. The enemy does not kill blindly, savagely, like a dog frothing at the mouth, but kills methodically, like a robot, measuring height, weight, years, setting aside plumbers and electricians while determining that doctors and nurses should die.

The enemy robs and kills, and the Jew, knowing that he is being killed only because he is a Jew, sanctifies G-d in going to his death, wants to die with the correct words on his lips, because the Jew, who sanctifies every atom of life, sanctifies dying as well; and a martyr's death must be accompanied by a blessing that is correct.

What do you say to a Jew who is a Jew unto death?

Can the modern Jew fathom it? Can the world fathom it? Can the German fathom it? Does one laugh perplexed? Does one gasp amazed? Because it is amazing, and at the same time it is a very basic question that requires an answer: What blessing do you recite when you are about to be martyred?

It is so elementary that tears are not enough.

Foreword

Sh'eilos UTeshuvos MiMa'makim — literally, "Questions and Responses from Out of the Depths" — originated in the ghetto of Kovno, in Slobodka, where I survived the Holocaust. During those dark years I noted down, in pencil, on scraps of paper torn from concrete sacks, the questions asked of me by my fellow Jews, and the answers I gave them, concerning problems of Jewish religious observance amidst the hardships and dangers of ghetto life. I placed these notes into tin cans, which I buried in the soil of the ghetto in the hope that they would be found after the war and serve as a historic record of how, no matter what befell, the Jews of the Kovno ghetto were determined to live by the laws of the Torah.

After the liberation of Kovno in August, 1944, I unearthed these cans and found their contents happily intact. Now began the arduous work of deciphering and editing my own scribbled notes. The product of my labors was a series of five volumes, published one at a time, under the title, **Sh'eilos UTeshuvos MiMa'amakim.** The Rabbinic authorities who have studied these volumes have described them as a unique document immortalizing the spiritual greatness demonstrated by Jews during the Holocaust.

This book, **Responsa From The Holocaust,** is an abridged English version of the original five-volume series. In order to condense the material from five volumes into one book of manageable size, the more detailed Halakhic explanations and references on which my responses were based had to be omitted. My responses of course, are stated in full. Obviously, **Responsa From The Holocaust** is not intended as a reference work for Rabbinic scholars, who in any event, have access to the five Hebrew volumes. This English version is meant primarily for laymen, and for students of Jewish history seeking an insight into the spiritual concerns that engaged religious Jews in one of the ghettos of Nazi Europe.

The motivations that impelled me to undertake this English translation are very personal. To paraphrase the Prophet Jeremiah, "I am a man who saw the affliction." I myself lived through the events described in the questions and responses recorded in this book. And I want my fellow Jews, and the rest of the world, to know, and never to forget, the bestiality unleashed by Hitler and his cohorts upon mankind in the guise of modern civilization and technical skill. Despite the abundant surviving documentary and visual evidence that the ovens and gas chambers were no figments of sick minds, books have been written by individuals who deny that Hitler ever killed six million Jews, and there is always the danger that, forty years after the fact, such authors might find gullible audiences. This is all the more reason for us to "remember what Amelak did to you... Do not forget."

In a more positive vein, my purpose is to add to the records of history my own experience of how the victims of the Nazi murderers demonstrated their superiority to the "master race" by clinging to God and to His Law in the midst of unspeakable sufferings. The inquiries on Jewish law and practice to which I had to respond were neither academic questions posed by scholars nor scenarios proposed by eccentrics playing theoretical games of "What if...?" They were made by ordinary Jews who refused to be turned into animals in instinctive search of bare survival and tenaciously upheld their obligation under the Divine Covenant: to observe to the best of their ability, even in the ghetto, the commandments of God's Torah, the Divine blueprint of true human civilization.

I wish to express my deep-felt thanks to one who is a pillar of the Jewish community and who, on his own initiative made possible the preparation of this volume: my own cousin, Harold Oshry. May God bless him, his wife, Claire, and his entire family with a long life of good health, accomplishment and contentment.

Ephraim Oshry
New York, N.Y.
Tammuz 5743 (June 1983)

Lithuania and Its Jews

Background to the Establishment
of the Kovno Ghetto

When Czarist Russia collapsed during World War I, liberated Lithuania was reconstituted an independent republic. Upon Lithuania's resurrection, the Jews wholeheartedly rejoiced. Full of deep feeling and respect for the liberated republic, they bent their energies to its reconstruction, taking a major share in its upbuilding and its success.

It seemed in fact that the Lithuanians appreciated that, and that the good relations developed then would create a new epoch of conviviality between the Jews and the gentiles who had lived together for so many centuries, had shared so many good and hard times, and had together attained national independence.

The little land of Lithuania lies along the eastern coast of the Baltic Sea. Its capital is Kovno (Kaunas). When the city of Vilna was annexed to it in 1939, the total population reached 3 million of whom 250,000 were Jews.

The Jewish settlement in Lithuania reached back some 700 years. In the 17th century, Lithuania became known as the greatest Jewish Torah center in Europe. Thanks to Lithuania's great Torah scholars and world-famous yeshivos, the country was labeled "the second Eretz Yisroel" and Vilna was renowned as "the Jerusalem of Lithuania."

Among the Torah giants who lived in Lithuania were: Rav Shabsy Cohen (*Shach*); Rav Moshe Rivkas (*B'eir Hagola*); Rav Eliyohu (the Gaon) of Vilna; Rav Chayim of Volozhin; Rav Yisroel of Salant; Rav Meir Simcha Cohen;

Rav Yosef Rosen; Rav Yisroel Meir Kagan (*Chofetz Chayim*); Rav Eliyohu Boruch Kamai of Mir; Rav Moshe Mordechai Epstein of Slobodka; and Rav Boruch Ber Leibowitz of Kamenitz. Among its great world-renowned yeshivos were: Volozhin, Mir, Slobodka, Radun, Telz, Kelm, and Ponievezh. Students from all over the world flocked to these yeshivos which made Lithuania famous as the major Torah center for Jewry.

Lithuania was also world-renowned for the *mussar* system developed and introduced by Rav Yisroel Lipkin of Salant.

Besides, Lithuania was renowned as the home of the greatest Jewish thinkers and leaders. Every creative Jewish approach either originated amid Lithuanian Jewry or ripened there. There is almost no important Jewish movement to which Lithuanian Jews did not contribute their share.

Over and above this all, Lithuanian Jewry was world-renowned for its hospitality, generosity, dedication, and love of Jews. There was a valid basis for the expression *"Litvak tzeilem kup* (Lithuanian Jew with the crucifix head)" because a Lithuanian Jew would stretch himself *"in der leng un in der breit* (horizontally and vertically)" to help a fellow-Jew.

An illustration of concentrated hospitality beyond the means of the hosts took place from late 1939 to early 1941 when Lithuanian Jewry hosted refugees from Poland, Germany, and other lands as they fled the advancing German armies. The warmth and brotherhood demonstrated by ordinary Lithuanians has been recorded by many of these survivors.

Such was Lithuania, the land of Torah wisdom and love of Jewry. This all existed — and is gone forever.

Lithuania, at the outset of its independent existence, did indeed give the Jews national autonomy in the form of independent Jewish communities under a national committee, an independent government-supported Jewish school system that taught in Yiddish and in Hebrew and over all this a Jewish ministry headed by a Jewish minister.

Lithuania could definitely have served for many other lands as a model of how to treat minorities.

But the sweet dream faded swiftly. The antisemitic element in the government brought down this institutional structure, and all that remained by the time World War Two broke out was the cultural autonomy — the religious and secular school systems under Jewish control.

In the economic sector the Lithuanians soon displayed their appreciation of the Jewish contribution by forcing them out of their long-held positions, by making life generally difficult for the Jews, and by compelling them to emigrate.

The climax came in 1941 when the Lithuanians attacked the Jews with shocking cruelty, tortured and murdered them, killing innocent infants and the unfortunate ill in indescribably horrible ways.

The German murderers finished the job. Together with their Lithuanian assistants they uprooted the centuries-old Jewry of Lithuania. A bloody tidal wave of mass butchery passed over Lithuanian Jewry and swept away all the yeshivos and all the other communal institutions. Horrifying suffering was the common lot of that Jewry's leaders and sages and its masses.

The behavior of the Lithuanians to the Jews is an eternal Cain-sign. See how they treated the Jews they had lived with for 700 years! See how they treated the Jews who had invested their marrow and blood into rebuilding Lithuania!

My precious Jewish Lithuania, how can I forget you? How can I live in peace when your fearsome destruction is still vivid in my mind? Like Jeremiah I cry, "Let my head be water and my eyes a spring of tears, so that I can bewail day and night the murdered of my people!"

The Destruction Begins

"I am the man who saw tribulation by the rod of His wrath." I witnessed the destruction and annihilation of Lithuanian Jewry. I saw the ruin and horrors suffered by every individual family and personally suffered the entire

Hell of suffering and bondage imposed by the Germans on our Jews. I, too, drank from the cup of hemlock.

Thank G-d, I survived the murderers. I am one of the very few surviving Lithuanian Jews.

How was I saved? I do not know. That was G-d's wish. In what merit? I surely do not know. It was the will of the Master of the universe that I survive the evil and leave that Hell in one piece.

That was real Hell. Whoever has not lived under German rule cannot imagine it, cannot conceive what happened to us in Lithuania during the awful years between the German occupation and the liberation of Lithuania by the Red army on the first of August 1944. Any comparison to the life of a dog or a wild animal misses the mark.

This Hell lasted three years. In the course of those horrifying years almost the entire blooming Jewish community of Lithuania was wiped out. Gone were the yeshivos, the tents of Torah and scholarship; gone were the Jewish communities and their institutions; gone were the Jewish journals; gone up in smoke were the Jewish libraries; uprooted were the over-the-centuries rooted Jewish communities. The ancient tree of Lithuanian Jewry was chopped down and its trunk forever uprooted.

The survivors were "one from a city and two from a clan," witnesses of the terrible destruction, orphaned and mourning — surviving, must be, in order to transplant to other soil the Torah of the Lithuanian yeshivos, "so that Torah will not be forgotten by Jews." And also, perhaps, to relate. So that children and grandchildren will remember, will never forget what the Amalekites did to us — all the Amalekites, German and Lithuanian alike.

Yes, I am a witness of this destruction without peer in the history of our people.

The destruction of Lithuania. I feel it my duty to relate here the *megilah* of this awful destruction. We must relate it. Let people know what happened!

The Seventh and Ninth Forts

In anticipation of war with Germany, at the turn of the century, the Russian Czars constructed a chain of forts to serve as a "Maginot Line" against the Germans. These forts were built in valleys and on hills along Russia's Lithuanian border with Prussia. Thousands of people worked at building them and millions of rubles were spent on them. During the First World War, those forts were as helpful to Russia as the Maginot Line was to France. The Seventh Fort and the Ninth were built near Slobodka-Kovno.

Who could have imagined that the Seventh and Ninth Forts would ever play so horrible a role in the history of Jewry in Lithuania? For they became death camps for Lithuanian Jews and also for at least 40,000 German, Austrian, Czechoslovakian and French Jews.

Lithuanian Bloodbath

My first memories of the German occupation of Lithuania are the worst. I cannot free myself of them till this very day. How many years have passed since the awful night of June 25, 1941, when the Lithuanian fifth column, the shaulists, fascists who looked forward to Hitler's invasion of Lithuania, celebrated their victory with a bloodbath of the Jews in the old, proud Jewish citadel of Torah — Slobodka.

It was a Wednesday night, several days after the outbreak of the Russo-German war. We were expecting terrible suffering, but none of us imagined that what would happen to us under the German occupation would be as frightening or as horrifying as it really turned out. All our imaginings about the Nazi terror turned out pale and unreal when measured against what actually took place.

Another shocking surprise for us was the position taken by the Lithuanian populace — our "good" Christian neighbors. There was literally not one gentile among the Christians of Slobodka who openly defended a Jew at a time when Slobodka's ten thousand Jews, with whom they had lived together all their lives, were threatened with the most horrible pogrom imaginable.

Not everything can be told, not every one of the horrors that took place that night in Slobodka. But even what I shall relate here is enough to show how great was the cruelty of our neighbors, how it served as a fitting prelude to the ultimate cruelty of the German annihilators. This unspeakable cruelty is unmatched in human history.

That Wednesday, as night fell, the Shaulist Lithuanian fascists accompanied by groups of ordinary Lithuanians, marched into the Jewish neighborhood of Slobodka armed with hatchets and saws. They began the pogrom on Jurborg Street, going from house to house, from apartment to apartment, murdering people by the most horrible deaths — men, women, and children — old and young. They hacked off heads, sawed people through like lumber, prolonging the agony of their victims as long as possible.

The butchers' first visit was to the apartment of Mordechai Yatkunsky and his wife Dr. Stein-Yatkunsky. They murdered them and their son most horribly: they hacked off hands, feet, and other organs — human fantasy cannot imagine the scene of horror we found on Jurborg Street. They chopped off the head of the Rabbi of Slobodka, Rav Zalman Ossowsky — G-d, avenge him! — and placed it in a window with a sign "THIS IS WHAT WE'LL DO TO ALL THE JEWS." They did just that. They killed all Jews — rabbis, professionals, zionist activists, communists — any Jew they got their hands on. From Jurborg Street they proceeded to Yatkever Street and beyond. The carnage was indescribable.

From all the streets chilling screams were heard, and above all sounds came the ancient ultimate cry, "Shma Yisroel!"

We, the Jews in hiding, could not find repose. How we "lucky ones" who were not killed that night felt, is something every Jew with a Jewish heart can easily imagine.

The most shocking, perhaps, of all the acts of butchery on that night when so many ordinary, precious Jews were put to death so cruelly, was the martyring of the Rabbi of Slobodka, Rav Zalman, may his mention be a blessing. The murderers bound him to a chair, put his head on his open Gemora and sawed his head off. They then cruelly killed his son, the young genius Rabbi Yudel Ossowsky, and shot the Rabbi's wife. Of all those at home that day, only the Rabbi's 5-year-old granddaughter Esther survived by hiding under a bed. Tragically Esther was later killed with her mother, Rochel, on Friday, Setember 26, 1941.

When we entered the house we found the severed heads of the Rabbi and his son lying separately. Rav Zalman's headless body was still "sitting" in his rabbinic armchair and the Talmud volume at his place was open to Tractate *Nida*, folio 33. The martyr had been studying when the beasts entered. How Rav Yudel looked is impossible for me to describe; I have no words for it.

That terror-filled night the murderers also killed the sexton of the Slobodka Yeshiva, Reb Gershon. With his throat slit, not yet dead, he lay there and chortled, "Children, when you are freed, tell about our suffering and hell!"

Another wounded Jew, tossing in his death agonies, wrote in blood on the wall, "Revenge." This inscription remained untouched for a long while.

Jews threw themselves from the bridge into the Viliya River, in order to save themselves. And the murderers took pot-shots at them from the bridge.

Besides these martyrs, many well-known Jews were murdered that night, among them the brilliant Reb Yona Karpilov of Minsk. The Shaulists tore out his internal organs, wrapped them in a *tallis* (prayer shawl) and placed them next to the body of the murdered *tzadik* (righteous man). A large number of Slobodka Yeshiva students were killed that night.

When the murderers had completed their "work" in the houses, they took to shooting and butchering in the streets. At the intersection of Jurborg Street and Shosei they shot the blacksmith, then lined up 26 Jews against the wall and shot them. Anyone they caught in the street — man, woman, or child — was butchered. They let no one through alive. At the bridge leading to Kovno they buried 34 Jews alive.

We, a group of rabbis and yeshiva students, were hiding that night in the home of the spiritual director of the Slobodka Yeshiva, Rabbi Avrohom Grodzinsy. With us was the great sage Rabbi Elchonon Wasserman. We passed that night in prayer and tears. But we also discussed what to do.

Mr. Abraham Drushkovitch came in and described what was taking place. We concluded that the murderers had decided to annihilate all the Jews. What could we do? What plan could we follow? That was the question that tormented all of us that night when Jewish heads were rolling in the streets of Slobodka. We could come up with no plan of action.

The next morning all the martyrs were buried in a mass grave in the cemetery. The Jews decided on this step despite all the dangers that threatened them.

I do not believe I shall ever be able to erase that fearsome night from my memory, the night that marked the beginning of Lithuania's destruction.

Kovno's Jews Driven into the Ghetto

June and July 1941 were months of bloody terror in Jewish Lithuania. During those two months Jews were murdered and tortured day and night. Thousands of Jews — men, women, and children — young and old, were killed in the weirdest ways. Naturally, looting and plundering were the order of the day. Yet — despite the murdering — those two months were an idyll compared to what later took place. True, Jews were robbed and murdered in those months, but the bloody terror was unorganized; it was unsystematic, unplanned. That was specifically a Lithuanian terror — a "prank" directed against the Jews by their "good" Lithuanian neighbors rather than a planned program of annihilation following the German system.

The most horrible aspect of his whole story of murder and plunder was that we Jews could not even then perceive the handwriting on the wall, that this bloody scenario was only the prologue to a great tragedy. As bloody as the prologue was, there were Jews who believed everything would quiet down.

That was perhaps not a question of false security as much as one of carelessness and lack of foresight. The Germans themselves — and their agents — spread rumors that the Germans were planning to bring order to everything. We all knew that the Germans were systematic people, and they themselves declared, "We Germans consider you Jews our enemies. We will therefore deprive you of all rights and declare you pariahs, turn you into slave-laborers. You will labor for us the way slaves labor for their masters, and if you obey no harm will befall you."

This was how the Germans addressed the leaders of the Jewish community council, the Eltestenrat they themselves appointed. The Eltestenrat was, of course, chosen to facilitate the carrying out of the Germans' heinous plans. But not all of us sensed that the council was no more than an instrument for German plans.

Not everyone wished to or could believe that the Germans were capable of genocide as they ultimately showed. People consoled themselves with weakness drops. Eternal Jewish optimism helped along — but here the optimism bordered on irresponsibiliity and credulousness.

In the midst of the bloody Lithuanian terror, Jews hoped and believed it would abate; an end had to come to it, they claimed; how long can such a bloodbath last? And we, the Jews of faith, certainly prayed and hoped for G-d's help. Among us, the Jews of faith, the feeling ran strongly that a divine decree had been issued and sealed, that in the natural scheme of things there was no hope for a speedy termination. We sensed, perceived that the worst was yet to come, the sufferings that precede redemption.

The period of bloody street terror did indeed come to an end. Here and there attacks and murders took place; Jew-murder never stopped. But the general terror of the first month or two passed. And a new period, the period of annihilating Jews systematically, began. Not everyone recognized this, because it began under the guise of "organization," of introducing German orderliness. The Lithuanians very enthusiastically helped exterminate the Jews, and continued to do so throughout the Occupation period. But the orders came from the Germans. The detailed German program for the extermination of European Jewry was applied in Lithuania.

In our case, as everywhere else under bloody German control in Europe, the process began with *Aussiedlung*. That was the term the Germans used for transferring Jews from their hometowns and resettling them in concentrated areas such as work camps and ghettoes. Later it came to mean taking them to extermination camps.

I think the original term used at the very outset was *Ubersiedlung*, which meant simply relocating Jews from one area into other quarters. That was the period when the ghettoes were created. In Kovno, the *Ubersiedlung* into the ghettoes began on July 15, 1941. This date marks the beginning of the tragic end of Lithuanian Jewry.

On that day the Jews of Kovno began to move into the ghettoes that were created in Kovno's suburb, Slobodka. Tragically, both ghettoes in Slobodka for the Jews of Kovno were built by Jews. Young Jewish men, slave-workers, built them, unaware for what purpose they were building those ghettoes.

By that time, Kovno's Jews had already registered in the Labor Office, unaware that they had really registered with the Angel of Death. The Germans wanted every name so that they could systematically annihilate every Jew — so that there would be no survivors. But the Jews, at first, had no notion of this.

Two ghettoes were set up in Slobodka, the Big Ghetto and the Little Ghetto. The Big Ghetto held 27,500 Jews while the Little Ghetto held 2,500. Everything was done systematically. The two ghettoes were linked by a long, wooden overhead footbridge, over which the subdued Jews ran up and down to get from the Big Ghetto to the Little

Ghetto. The ghettoes were stongly guarded; guards were stationed two meters apart — German and Lithuanian soldiers. The Jews were forced into the ghettoes like animals being penned prior to slaughter. They went on foot — men, women and children. As they went they were abused. Every day the march of the dead went on from Kovno to Slobodka.

Even when the Jews were entering the ghettoes, many of us still believed we might yet be saved. The Germans told us that things were going to be "good " for us. They convinced many Jews that they would have their "own government," that they would be strictly among their own kind; all they would have to do is work. Some Germans spoke earnestly, others derisively. But the miserable Jews grasped at every straw of hope, "Perhaps, maybe, hopefully, we'll survive the bad times. Perhaps it *will* be limited to back-breaking labor."

That's how the Jews talked. Few felt the noose tightening around their necks.

To make room for all the Jews in the two ghettoes, the Lithuanians had to move out of their Slobodka homes and move into homes vacated by Jews in Kovno, or into those sections of Slobodka not included in the ghettoes. In any event, there was not enough room for the 30,000 Jews of Kovno. As a result, the synagogues and *batey midrash* were turned into living quarters, the smallest space becoming suddenly very valuable. Those who could afford it paid large indemnities to the Lithuanians moving out to get their apartments.

Worst off were those who did not have the means of getting themselves some sort of home. They meanwhile moved all their goods into the ghettos and left them with friends or acquaintances. In many streets lay sections of furniture, packages and parcels, and all kinds of household items which belonged to people too poor to find an attic or a cellar where they could deposit their few possessions.

In the very first week of the *Ubersiedlung*, the majority of the Jewish populace had moved into the ghettoes. The general attitude was reflected by comments such as, "Better in a ghetto, if that keeps the murderous forces at bay, so long as we don't have to hear their animal snarls." Or "Yes, it's hard, but at least we're among Jews."

Day after day carts crawled across the Slobodka bridge into the ghettoes. People gave up their homes of many years, their houses and their estates, and moved behind the barbed wire in order to be left in peace.

Behind the barbed wire, life entered a "normal" course with all the contradictions that implies. People lived each moment, temporarily ignoring the awesome peril of the catastrophe and hoping that time would bring relief.

At great personal risk, all the Torah scrolls were removed from the synagogues of Kovno, as were the sets of Talmud and other sacred works. We transferred the library of Rabbi Yitzchok Elchonon Spector, the world-famous Rabbi of Kovno, and also the city library. Everything was temporarily stored in rooms in the School of Agronomy which was within the ghetto confines.

On August 15, 1941, the Jews were finally driven into the ghettoes. We crowded into the poorest of accommodations; happy to be alive. New decrees streamed forth. We barely grew accustomed to one location and a new edict was issued: Move! We'd move from one street to the next, our territory constantly shrinking. We Jews were being driven like a flock of sheep being squeezed into a pen. The goals were to make our lives ever more miserable, to shame us in every way.

Given no alternative, even the most unnatural situation becomes tolerable. One accepts his fate, accepts the justice of G-d's will. All effort focuses on maintaining some stamina. One hopes for redemption even at the very edge of hallucination. The Jews were forced to put up barbed wire fences around the ghettoes.

Every person had a narrow space of his own, just about big enough for him to turn around in. The last Jews leaving Kovno were robbed of their furniture by the Germans and their helpers, who scoffed at their despondent and suffering victims. They tortured them with derision, "You don't need so much furniture!" "You won't be needing any where you're going!" The Lithuanians in particular called out, "You can leave it with us for when you return from the ghettoes. We'll keep it for you. We'll take good care of it and there will be nothing missing." In the end, the Lithuanian bloodhounds got none of it. The Germans loaded it all into railroad cars and shipped it off to Germany for their own homes.

The *Ubersiedlung* ended August 15. For 30 days the Jews had marched through the streets, some of them collapsing along the way.

Thus did the curtain fall on the history of Jewish Kovno, mother-city of Judaism, the city of Rabbi Yitzchok Elchonon, the city of yeshivos, of Torah, of old and modern Jewish culture. All were driven out. Not one Jew remained in Kovno after August 15.

Kovno, Jewish Kovno, the Kovno we all remember, came to an end on August 15, 1941. Who knows if Kovno will ever come to life again? I fear it is gone forever, for the Jews who have returned there are merely dry bones who will never restore the Kovno of yore.

Several Jewish monuments remain in Kovno: the Reform Temple, and several other buildings such as Hoisman's Kloiz, which is the community center.

But living Jews are no longer there.

PHOTOGRAPHS

1. *MOVING INTO THE GHETTO.* Kovno was occupied by the Germans on June 24, 1941. On July 11, an order was issued to the effect that between July 15 and August 15, 1941, all the city's Jews were to move into a ghetto set up in Slobodka.

2. ENTRANCE TO THE GHETTO. The ghetto set up in Slobodka for the Jews of Kovno initially housed a population of almost 30,000. But of these, some 13,000 were murdered already during the first months of the ghetto's existence, mainly at the Seventh and Ninth Forts.

3. THE GHETTO BRIDGE. The Kovno ghetto was divided into two parts, the Big Ghetto and the Little Ghetto. The two ghettos were linked by a wooden bridge that was heavily guarded by Germans and Lithuanians.

4. JEWS AT THE SEVENTH FORT. Soon after the German occupation of Kovno, about 10,000 Jews were seized in various sections of the city and taken to the Seventh Fort, a part of the city's ancient fortifications. Between 6,000 and 7,000 of these Jews were murdered early in July 1941.

5. THE NINTH FORT near Slobodka, the end of the road for inmates of the Kovno ghetto and thousands of Jewish deportees from Germany, France and other Nazi-occupied countries. Jews imprisoned in the Ninth Fort were either murdered on the spot or sent on to death camps.

6. UMSIEDLUNGSAKTION (OPERATION RESETTLEMENT): Jews about to be deported from the Kovno ghetto. In two such **Aktionen** in 1942, Jews were transferred from the Kovno ghetto to the ghetto of Riga, Latvia. In October 1943, about 3,000 additional Jews were deported from the Kovno ghetto to concentration camps in Estonia.

7. LIFE IN THE KOVNO GHETTO. Jews with the Star of David plainly visible on their outer clothing.

8. LEADERS OF THE KOVNO GHETTO. The **Altestenrat** (Council of Jewish. Elders). Seated in the center is the chairman, Dr. Elhanan Elkes, a physician. After the liquidation of the ghetto, Dr. Elkes was deported to Dachau, where he died on July 25, 1944, a week before the liberation of Kovno.

9. THE GHETTO POLICE. The Jewish police force responsible for the maintenance of order in the Kovno ghetto under the supervision of the **Altestenrat** (Council of Jewish Elders). This police force helped some 250 armed Jewish fighters escape from the ghetto and join partisan units in the woods outside Kovno.

10. MUTUAL ASSISTANCE IN THE KOVNO GHETTO. Ghetto inmates reading an appeal for used clothing: "Jews Donate for the poor and the naked — old winter clothing and shoes you no longer need! Do not stint! Give generously!".

11. COLLECTING "ARTIFACTS OF THE EXTINCT JEWISH RACE." Nazi postwar plans included exhibits of Jewish books and ceremonial objects as "artifacts of the extinct Jewish race." To this end, the Germans ordered the collection of all Jewish books in the ghettos, to be stored in warehouses until the exhibits could be organized. Here, ghetto children attempt to rescue books about to be carted off to the warehouse in the Kovno ghetto. Rabbi Oshry served for a time as custodian of this warehouse. This position gave him a unique opportunity to protect the books from desecration. Perhaps even more important, it afforded him access to major works of Rabbinic literature which he used as references in the formulation of his **teshuvot** (responsa) to questions on Jewish religious observances in the ghetto.

12. GRAFFITI ON A WALL IN THE KOVNO GHETTO. "Jews! Take Revenge!"

13. THE KOVNO GHETTO IN FLAMES. In July 1944, as Soviet forces approached Kovno, the Germans liquidated the ghetto, using grenades and explosives to kill Jews hiding in the ghetto's bunkers. About 8,000 Jews were sent from the ghetto to concentration camps in Germany proper. Over 80 percent of them died before the end of Hitler's Third Reich.

14. AFTER THE LIQUIDATION OF THE GHETTO. Bodies of

Jews massacred during the liquidation of the Kovno ghetto in July 1944.

15. THE NINTH FORT. Piles of dead Jews placed on gasoline-soaked stacks of wood for cremation. Russian forces arrived in Kovno before the Germans could finish the cremations.

16. SURVIVORS. In front of the ghetto bunker in which he survived, an engineer, Indursky (left, front), explains to Red army Major Bulganov (in uniform, at right) how the bunker was built. Rabbi Oshry (beardless, in dark jacket) is standing between Indursky and Major Bulganov.

17. AFTER LIBERATION. A group of partisans and Jewish survivors at the Ninth Fort, August, 1944. Rabbi Oshry (wearing a hat) is in the center.

18. THE AFTERMATH. German prisoners are forced to help bury the Jewish dead in the ghetto cemetery.

19. TRIBUTE TO THE DEAD. Rabbi Oshry (in tallith), flanked by Jewish partisans, eulogizes the martyrs of the ghetto on the grounds of the Ninth Fort.

20. "BRANDS PLUCKED FROM THE FIRE." Children who survived the war in hiding with Gentile families. The survivors of the Kovno ghetto gathered up these children and restored them to the Jewish community.

1941

Outrage
Begins

1: *Endangering Yourself to Save Another*

Question: When the Germans entered Lithuania on 28 Sivan 5701 — June 23, 1941 — they immediately began to display their great barbarity toward the Jews with all kinds of evil and abominable acts. Day after day they hunted Jewish men and women in the streets of Kovno, and sent them to the Seventh Fort where their fate was determined. The accursed evildoers were abetted by the Lithuanians who were pleased at the opportunity to openly hunt the Jews whom they had always hated.

As the Talmud says, "Whoever makes trouble for the Jews becomes a leader." Among the Lithuanians, there were some who excelled in their cruelty toward the Jews, particularly when they sought to find favor in the eyes of their German masters. Secure in their knowledge of the Lithuanians' hatred, the Germans appointed them to positions of power and authority in hunting down Jews. These Lithuanians caused the Jews great anguish, robbing and murdering no less than the Germans. Hundreds of Jews were taken captive at that time on the streets and from their homes — among them a great number of yeshiva students.

In those horror-filled days I was asked by our master, the great *gaon*[1] and *tzadik*[2], Rav Avrohom Grodzinsky — may G-d avenge his death —the Director of the Slobodka Yeshiva, to go to Rabbi David Itzkovitch, the secretary of the Agudath Harabonim, and ask him to approach the Lithuanians in charge of the Jewhunts, whom he knew from before the war, and to persuade them to free the yeshiva students.

1. Sage
2. Righteous man

1

The question that arose was whether he was permitted by Halacha to approach the Lithuanians about liberating the yeshiva students, for they could just as easily take him captive as any other Jew. Was he allowed to endanger his own life in order to save fellow-Jews?

Response: By the strict interpretation of Halacha one could not obligate Rabbi Itzkovitch to endanger himself in order to save the yeshiva students. Yet if, as a sensitive man of spirit, he would volunteer to endanger himself on the chance that he might save them, he was certainly not to be stopped. Such a matter had to be studied very carefully. While not overly protecting himself, he was obligated to seek the means of fulfilling the statement of our Sages, "Whoever maintains a single Jewish life is considered as though he maintained the whole world." This was doubly true at a time when the enemy was determined to destroy the Jewish body and spirit together; for the maintenance of the Torah is dependent on the yeshiva students who dedicate their lives to studying it. The Germans and the Lithuanians poured out their fury upon the Torah leaders and blasphemed everything holy to the Jewish people. Even as they tortured and butchered the martyrs, they blasphemed the G-d of the Jews.

It was mandatory for every person who appreciated what was at stake to do everything in his power to save the yeshiva students so that the candle of G-d, the light of Torah, would not be extinguished. Only in this manner could we foil to some degree the evil plot to destroy the Torah and obliterate its memory from the world.

Rabbi Itzkovitch heeded my request and courageously made the effort on behalf of the yeshiva students. He succeeded in having the Lithuanians free the yeshiva students from their imprisonment. G-d! Remember this to his credit! And avenge his pure blood, which was later shed in an extermination camp.

2: *A Kohein[1] Who Was Forced to Convert*

Question: On 28 Sivan 5701 — June 23, 1941 — when the German troops set foot on Lithuanian soil, they began to murder Jewish people without mercy — infants, women, men, young and old. They tortured them, they stabbed them, and shot them — they did everything to exterminate them.

A man and his wife were killed on the same day by the accursed murderers. Their only son survived because their non-Jewish maid managed to hide him. The 16-year-old boy was greatly embittered by the evil that had befallen him; he felt alone in the world and feared that the gentile maid might report him to the German murderers.

With the passage of time, the maid could no longer hide him because she feared the Germans would discover she was hiding a Jewish boy and kill them both. To save him, she brought him to the priest of her church and made a deal — protection in exchange for baptism. The priest granted the maid's request, and later, when he had hidden the boy among the gentiles, the priest did not reveal to his parishioners that the boy was really a Jew. For a while, the boy lived without the fear of being harmed. He had everything he could possibly think of — everything except peace of mind.

Before his eyes he kept seeing the horror of the murders of his father and his mother, and his misery could not be placated by food or drink. Even at night his pain did not

1. Every descendant of Aaron, the brother of Moses, is a *Kohein* (plural, *Kohanim*).

3

abate; how could he sleep when he knew that his people were suffering and he was not suffering with them?

One day the boy gathered every ounce of courage he had, and left his comfortable place among the gentiles. He found his way back to the Kovno ghetto to live with his Jewish brethren and to share their fate. Ultimately the boy returned to the service of G-d with his entire heart and soul, and deeply regretted his baptism.

I was asked a threefold question. First: was it permissible to include this boy in a *minyan*[2] of ten? Second: Since the boy was a *kohein*, might he be called to the Torah to the *kohein's* reading ? Third: could he raise his hands in benediction in the tradition of his forefathers?

Response: If someone is forced to convert against his will, he is not considered a *mumar*, an apostate, but rather an *annus*, one who acted out of compulsion. This boy was certainly compelled to convert in order to save his life. As a consequence, it was permissible for him to be included in a *minyan* and to function as a *kohein* by reading first from the Torah and by raising his hands in benediction. By running away from the gentiles and rejoining his people within the ghetto walls, in the knowledge that he was risking certain death, demonstrated that he had preferred dying together with his brethren over living among non-Jews.

On the day the ghetto was destroyed in 5704 (1944), the Germans removed the last of the Jews who had survived previous selections, and put them to death. On that day, together with the rest of his martyred brethren, this holy lad was killed, fulfilling the verse, "Who were beloved and pleasant in their lifetimes and were not separated in death." May G-d recall him along with the rest of the righteous when He avenges the blood of His martyred servants.

2. A quorum.

3: *Shaving with a Razor*

Question: In our suffering under the hands of the accursed Germans who daily sought to cause us physical and mental anguish by their decrees of all kinds, one of the charges they laid against us was that Jews are filthy and carry all kinds of infectious diseases. They were especially furious with any Jew who wore a beard — which most Orthodox Jews did. When the accursed evildoers saw a bearded Jew, they immediately subjected him to ridicule and harassment, with death as a possible result. Intimidated, all the bearded ghetto dwellers removed their beards — even the rabbis and Torah sages; they realized it was absolutely impossible to leave their beards intact no matter how much they suffered internally at having to give up their emulation of the "divine image."

The Jewish leaders were compelled to remove their beards for another reason: A special goal of the Germans was the destruction of the Jewish leadership. A beard was seen by the Germans as identifying a rabbi, and the *Rabbiner* were singled out to be hounded mercilessly and killed outright. The rabbis were consequently constrained to remove their beards in order to protect their lives.

Only two people in the ghetto retained their beards. One was the rabbi of Kovno, Rabbi Avrohom DovBer Kahana-Shapira, who did not remove his beard because he was known to the Germans and stood to gain nothing by removing his beard. He therefore guarded the honor of Jewry by leaving his beard intact.

The second individual was one of the important householders in Kovno, a *chasid* of Chabad, Rav Feivel

5

Zussman, who took the risk involved and did not remove his beard. He managed to retain his Jewish pride and glory for a number of years — until the *Kinderakzion*[1] of 3 and 4 Nissan 5704 — March 27 and 28, 1944. On that day the Germans searched every single attic and basement, cave and tunnel, in order to find the unfortunate children whom they dragged out to be annihilated. G-d! Avenge their sacred, pure blood!

To facilitate transportation of ghetto laborers to the airfield outside Kovno, the Germans set up a camp for slave laborers outside Aleksot, the suburb of Kovno nearest the airfield. One of the Jews confined to this camp asked me what to do about his beard since in his camp there was no implement for removing his beard other than a razor blade. His question was whether he might be permitted to remove his beard with the razor because of the danger to his life.

Response: I ruled that he might shave with the razor since there is no disagreement among the authorities that it is permissible to remove one's beard with a razor to save one's life. There was not even a non-Jew available in the prisoner-of-war camp to shave this man so as to circumvent his being shaved by a Jew, whether himself or another. But even if there had been a non-Jew in the camp, it would have made no difference because the accursed Germans forbade non-Jews to help Jews in any way.

---

1. Children's purge.

4: *Making a Tahara[1] in Advance*

Question: On the night of the 25th of Menachem Ov 5701 —
August 18, 1941 — I was giving a Torah lecture at Aba
Yechezkel's Kloiz in Slobodka. This was after the German
invasion of Lithuania, and throughout the land the joy of the
Jewish people was being cut short by the Germans. In the
middle of the lecture, we suddenly heard heartbreaking
screaming and wailing. The daughter-in-law of one of the
regular members of the class, Reb Zalman Sher — may G-d
avenge him — burst into the *kloiz* and gasped that the
Germans had, moments ago, killed her three sons together
with her husband, the son of Reb Zalman. Right then and
there, as she bewailed her four deaths, the woman's father-
in-law passed out, fell off the chair, and died before our eyes.

The director of the Chevra Kadisha (burial society), Reb
Chayim Moshe Kaplan — G-d, avenge him! — who was
responsible for arranging funerals in accord with Jewish
custom, posed the following problem to me: Since the
enemy's decrees affected the entire population — both the
living and the dead — it was impossible to know when the
funeral and burial would take place. Under the tragic
circumstances of the German invasion, there was no
question it would take at least a day or two, so it was possible
that by the time the funeral could be arranged there would be
no one available to perform the *tahara*, the ritual washing
and preparation of the body for burial usually performed just
before burial. Present in our *kloiz*, however, were a number of
close friends of Reb Zalman and it seemed best to extend

---

1. The preparation of a corpse for burial.

final respect to the departed by performing the *tahara* immediately — on the very table where the fallen Jew had studied Mishnayos and Gemara.

The question was simply, "Is it permissible to make the *tahara* in advance rather than as close to the funeral as possible?"

Response: I permitted immediate *tahara* for Reb Zalman. For future instances in the ghetto I instructed the director of the burial society, Reb Moshe Chayim, to perform the *tahara* for the deceased as soon as possible since no one could ever be certain that it would be possible to perform the *tahara* close to the time of burial.

5: *Jews Forced to Shred a Torah Scroll*

Question: On 4 Elul 5701 — August 27, 1941 — the Germans captured stray dogs and cats and brought them into the Neier Kloiz, a house of study in Slobodka — a suburb of the Lithuanian capital of Kovno, which the Germans turned into the ghetto of Kovno — where they shot them to death. But the grisly pleasure of the brutal murderers was not gratified with desecrating this sanctuary and turning it into a charnel house for the carcasses of dogs and cats. They proceeded to force a number of Jews to rip apart a Torah scroll with their own hands and to use the sheets of parchment to cover the carcasses of the shot animals. Other Jews were compelled to watch the Torah scroll being shredded and the Word of G-d defiled with the blood of these carcasses.

Subsequently, some of these witnesses came to the late rabbi of Kovno, Rabbi Avrohom DovBer Kahana-Shapira and asked him to arrange a program of penitence for all the Jews present during that tragic event, particularly those who were compelled to desecrate the Torah with their own hands. The ghetto dwellers who heard the report of this horrifying insult to the Torah, saw it as a sign that the fury of the Germans was being unleashed upon the entire community. It therefore seemed appropriate that all of us accept upon ourselves some form of penance and implore G-d to have mercy on His people and to tell Satan, "Enough!" Because the rabbi of Kovno was very ill then, he asked me to study the subject and to determine precisely what the people ought to do.

Response: Those who saw the scroll being torn were obligated to rend their garments. Those ghetto dwellers who did not see the act of depravity with their own eyes but only heard about it from others had no obligation to rend their garments.

Those who were forced to rend the Torah scroll with their own hands were obligated to fast, even though they had been forced to act at gunpoint. All those who witnessed this vile act also had to fast. But if they could not fast because of physical weakness due to the hunger and the other sufferings they bore daily in the ghetto, one could not obligate them to fast. Although the ghetto dwellers who were not present — who only heard about it from others — did not have to fast, they were nevertheless to contribute to charity whatever·they could afford to give.

On the Sabbath following the incident, I exhorted the community to examine their own deeds and to repent; particularly to accord proper respect to Torah scrolls and, especially, to Torah scholars. The rabbi of Kovno concurred with me in all this.

6: *Sabbath Torah Reading for Slave Laborers*

Question: On 16 Elul 5701 — September 8, 1941 — the accursed Germans issued an edict requiring the Jews of the Kovno Ghetto to supply 1,000 slave laborers to work in the nearby airfield, which was to be enlarged to accomodate large bombers. Previously, the Germans had been rounding up the 1,000 laborers themselves, but this edict ordered the Eltestenrat (the Council of Elders) of the ghetto to provide the 1,000 Jews every day.

Slave labor details went out every night and every day, and the unfortunate workers were compelled to labor even on the Sabbath. Great was their anguish when they whispered the Sabbath prayers while they stood digging in the ditches and trenches. With work tools in their hands, they welcomed the Sabbath queen, quietly singing *Lecho Dodi*, their hearts filled with hope and faith — the faith of the chosen people — that G-d would yet say, "You have sat too long in the vale of tears, the glory of G-d is about to be revealed to you."

The day-shift laborers finished work at 7:30 p.m. Although forced to violate the Sabbath, they still wanted to listen to the weekly Sabbath Torah readings normally read during the Sabbath morning prayers. The question that they faced was whether the Torah portion for that week could be read during the evening Mincha prayer, or whether it had to be read before Mincha. In addition, during the winter months when the days were short and they returned in total

11

darkness, the Sabbath long over, the question was whether it was at all possible to make up the reading of the Torah portion for that week?

Response: I ruled that on the long summer days when they completed their work in daylight, they were to read the portion of that Sabbath and then pray Mincha. During the short winter days, when they completed their work after the Sabbath had ended, there was no way for them to fulfill this mitzva.

Nevertheless, I told them that it was appropriate to make the effort to read the portion of the week from a Chumash[1] during the few moments that the accursed Germans allowed them for a lunch break, so as not to forget the mitzva of reading from the Torah on the Sabbath. This was done by a Jew named Reb Shimon, who prayed in the Merchants' Kloiz on Yavana Street in Kovno. In order to maintain the mitzva, he would read from a small Tanach[2] quietly during the lunch break.

1. Pentateuch
2. Bible

7: *Cooking on the Sabbath in the Ghetto*

Question: ' The accursed evildoers took 1,000 men every day for slave labor in the airfield outside the city of Kovno. One of my students, Reb Yaakov — may G-d avenge his death — came to me with the following problem.

He had the opportunity to work in the kitchen where they cooked the black soup *(jusnek)* that the Germans supplied the Jewish laborers along with 100 grams of bread every day. The problem was that he would be compelled to work there on Shaboss (the Sabbath) as well. One advantage to him, however, was that he would be spared the much more difficult slave labor at the airfield which was psychologically damaging as well as physically destructive. Simultaneously he would remain both physically and mentally healthier and would perhaps be able to survive the general starvation in the ghetto. Another aspect of his question was whether he might be allowed to eat on Shaboss of the soup that the himself had cooked on Shaboss.

Response: I ruled that he was allowed to cook on Shaboss, because the alternative of slave labor in the airfield on Shaboss was no less a desecration of the Sabbath than the cooking. In neither case would he be desecrating the Sabbath willfully, but solely out of compulsion. It was therefore preferable that he work in the kitchen because there he would get enough food to eat. I allowed him to eat the black soup that he himself would cook on Shaboss because it is not forbidden to eat the product of Shaboss labor where one eats it to preserve life.

8: *May a Person Save Himself by Causing the Death of a Fellow Jew?*

Question: On 16 Elul 5701 — September 8, 1941 — S.S. *Oberfuhrer* Goecke arrived in Lithuania and began the extermination of all the ghettos, including the Kovno Ghetto. His reputation as a bloodthirsty murderer preceded his arrival in Lithuania, stirring up great confusion among the ghetto occupants. As soon as he arrived, he began to execute Jews. And that was when the question of the white cards knows as *Jordan Schein* first came up.

The German commandant of the Kovno Ghetto, Jordan, had ordered the Eltestenrat, the council of elders, to distribute among the laborers in the ghetto 5,000 white cards, permits for the laborers to remain in the ghetto with their families, while the rest of the Jews were to be annihilated.

At that time the ghetto held some 30,000 Jews, among them 10,000 laborers. It is impossible to describe the confusion that broke out among the laborers, for every single one wanted a white card; without it, his family's fate was sealed.

The laborers encamped around the office of the Eltestenrat, many trying to grab the white cards by force.

On Wednesday, 25 Elul (September 17), when word got out that the Germans had the Jewish quarter surrounded, that armed guards had been placed at every exit, and that cannon had been emplaced around the ghetto walls, the confusion grew greater. Clearly, the Germans and their Lithuanian cohorts were getting ready to wipe out the Jews.

At the same time, word spread that armed Germans had burst into the homes of Jews in the Little Ghetto[1], expelling

1. See Question 10 for more details.

them with murderous fury. They lined them up on a plot of land in the business district where they separated the Jews into two groups: those who had white cards and those who did not. And there their families joined them in the respective lines.

Right then and there, in the midst of that confusion, I was asked a life-determining question. Was the Eltestenrat permitted to obey Jordan's order and accept cards and distribute them, or not? Every card that they distributed to a laborer automatically spelled a death sentence for another laborer. Did this mean that they were handing him over to the German murderers to be done with as they saw fit? In that case, they were choosing one life over another. On what basis could they determine whose life was more significant, who deserved a white card and who did not?

I was asked a second question too: Is it right for anyone to grab a white card to save his life? For by grabbing a *Jordan Schein* for yourself, you were sending another Jew and his family to death. How could you determine that your life was more valuable than another's?

Response: There are a number of views regarding the first question, some of which allow the Eltestenrat to hand out the white cards, and others which forbid it.

A similar incident took place several months later on 6 Marcheshvan 5702 — October 24, 1941 — in Kovno, where the Eltestenrat was ordered to post a notice in the streets of the ghetto that two days later, on October 26, all the inhabitants of the ghetto — men, women, and children, including the aged and the sick — were to gather in the Demokratiaplatz (Democracy Plaza) and that no Jew might remain at home at that time. The Eltestenrat immediately sent four people to the home of the Kovno rabbi, Rav Avrohom DovBer Kahana-Shapira, to ask whether they must obey the German order or not, because information they possessed indicated that a large percentage of the gathered would be put to death.

It was late at night when they came to the rabbi's house and the frail, old rabbi, seriously ailing, was already asleep.

Despite this, his wife woke him and told him about the delegation. He got out of bed immediately and was told the current situation in the ghetto. Upon hearing the gravity of the new decree, the rabbi began to tremble in anguish and almost passed out. It was necessary to give him a few drops of valerian. Recognizing the great responsibility that lay upon him, he told the delegation that Jewish history is long and bloody and replete with such evil decrees. Nevertheless he could not rule on the matter immediately; he needed some time. That night he did not return to his bed but searched through volumes dealing with the aspects of relevant *Halacha.* After lengthy deliberation, he ruled as follows: "If a decree is issued that a Jewish community be destroyed and a possibility exists to save some part of this community, the leaders of the community are obligated to gird themselves with the courage necessary to act with the fullest sense of the responsibility that lies upon them and to take every possible measure to save as many as can be saved."

I ruled similarly that it was the duty of the communal leaders to save as many people as possible. And since it was possible to save a number of people by issuing the white cards, the Eltestenrat had to take courage and distribute those cards in any way they saw fit to save as many people as possible.

And as to the question of laborers grabbing cards forcibly from other laborers, it would initially seem that no Jew is ever allowed to do anything that places another Jew's life in danger. Nevertheless, according to the principle outlined in answer to the first question, that in a case of danger to a community one must save whoever can be saved, it seemed that each laborer was entitled to do whatever he could to save his life and that of his family.

9: *Using the Garments of Martyred Jews*

Question: On the day before Rosh Hashana 5702 —
September 21, 1941 — due to the impending holy day, the
ghetto Jews did not fill the quota of 1,000 slave laborers
demanded by the Germans. The murderers were furious. Led
by their bloodthirsty chieftain Neumann, may his name be
obliterated, they entered the ghetto toward nightfall to grab
Jews for slave labor. They began by molesting and ended
with shooting two of them. They were merciless, particularly
toward those Jews who were in synagogues, having come in
to pray to G-d, to beg and supplicate Him to have mercy on
His suffering Jewish people. The two men who were shot
that Erev Rosh Hashana by the murderers were Yitzchok
Baum, owner of a metal shop on Linkova Street in Slobodka,
and Berel Mendelevitch, may G-d avenge their blood!

After the murderers had done their dirty work, they
ordered the Jews to dig a grave for the corpses and then to
remove the garments of the dead as a macabre gift for the
Jews who had dug the grave. I was asked whether these
garments, which had no bloodstains on them, might be put
to use or whether it was forbidden to make use of them.

Response: The Halacha *(Shulchan Aruch Yoreh Deah,
364:4)* is that if a Jew is found murdered, he is to be buried as
he was found without burial shrouds; not even his shoes are
to be removed. This applies to one who died with his
garments on. One who is murdered by non-Jews, even
though his blood has stopped flowing by the time he is found,
is still buried as found so as to arouse Divine anger.

Since the garments in our case had no blood upon them,

one might certainly use them and there would be no need to bury them with the corpses, were it not for the stated purpose of arousing Divine anger. Since the dead men had already been buried without their garments, the greatest pleasure one could provide them was to allow their surviving children to benefit from these garments, either by wearing them to warm themselves or by selling them in order to purchase food for survival. It seemed to me that it certainly would be the wish of the martyrs that the garments be given to their children to help them survive despite the efforts of the accursed murderers.

10: *Blowing a Cracked Shofar*[1]

Question: On the day before Rosh Hashana of 5702 I was asked on behalf of people in the camp near the town of Koshedar whether, in the absence of any other shofar, they could fulfill the obligation of hearing the shofar on Rosh Hashana by blowing a slightly cracked shofar.

Response: Most of the codifiers maintain that if less than half the shofar is cracked, it may be used. All the more so in this situation where no other shofar was available. I also considered the fact that these Jews were seeking to fulfill a mitzva while still alive, not knowing what the morrow would bring.

1. Ram's horn.

11: *Bringing Tefilin¹ into a Hospital Where All Personal Objects Are Burned*

Question: Among the sufferings imposed on the prisoners of the ghetto, the Germans introduced special horrors for the sick and the weak. Bloodthirsty, they poured down edict after edict upon the head of Jacob; they wanted to see Jewish people drown in a sea of Jewish blood and tears. And yet, no matter how much suffering they melted out, the fiends always came up with some new scheme to make the Jews suffer even more.

One of their devilish plots was unique: Its ostensible purpose was to give hope to the sick and the weak who had given up on life when they realized that there was no medicine available. The Germans, to confuse the sick even more, allowed them a glimmer of hope. They announced the establishment of a hospital in the Little Ghetto of Kovno. Alongside this small ghetto, there was another, larger ghetto; the two were connected by a wooden bridge. The pleasure this hospital gave the sadistic German enemy is beyond our imagination; simply, though, it was intended to raise the hopes of the weakest Jews by luring them into the German trap and then smashing them.

I was asked to render a halachic decision on the following problem: A boy whose leg the Germans had amputated lay in the hospital. Wishing to pray daily to his Creator, he sent a request through Jewish channels that a pair of *tefilin* be sent into the hospital. A persistent rumor in the ghetto claimed

---

1. *Tefilin*, phylacteries, are worn on one's head and arm in fulfilment of *Exodus* 13: 9 and 16, and *Deuteronomy* 6: 8 and 11: 18.

that the Germans burned each patient's personal possessions upon his death or dismissal. Knowing what might happen to the *tefilin,* was it still permissible to send a pair into the hospital?

Response: I ruled that the *tefilin* might be sent to the lad so that he could fulfill the Torah's commandment, in the merit of which G-d would not allow the *tefilin* to be destroyed. The story of the Germans burning personal effects was an unsubstantiated rumor, one of many produced by the fear that reigned in the ghetto. If we had known it to be a fact, I would definitely have forbidden sending him the *tefilin.* But a rumor alone was not enough to deprive that lad from praying with *tefilin.* They were sent through a trustworthy emissary who gave them to the boy secretly, away from German eyes.

I also felt that the *tefilin* would be an inspiration to the boy, a recent *baal teshuva* who had changed his life around from non-observance to observance, and make him feel part of the Jewish people. Dr. Davidovitch, who worked in the hospital, testified to the boy's great joy when he donned the *tefilin* for the first time.

On 3 Tishrey 5702 — September 23, 1941 — when the accursed Germans destroyed the Little Ghetto, they also burned down this hospital, incinerating the patients, nurses, and doctors inside. Some 60 Jews, including Dr. Davidovitch and the boy to whom the *tefilin* had been sent, were killed in the fire. G-d, avenge their blood!

Wonder of wonders! One of the Jews who had been inside the hospital was miraculously saved, and told us what happened before the incineration. The boy had guarded the *tefilin* literally with his life. When he realized that the hospital would be destroyed together with its patients and its staff, he asked this man to make every effort to hide the *tefilin* so that they would not fall into the hands of the defiling evildoers who would destroy them. The man succeeded in escaping from the hospital trap and showed us the treasure, the boy's *tefilin* that had been saved. May G-d fulfill in our time the verse, "For You, O G-d, have set it afire, and You will restore it through fire."

12: *Eventual Danger to Life*

Question: Beginning Elul 5701 — September 1941 — the Jews of Kovno were compelled to work in the airfield next to the city by the Germans who ordered the ghetto Jews to provide 1,000 men daily. Every one of the slave laborers was allowed one bowl of non-kosher soup as his daily ration plus 100 grams of bread. Many of the laborers understandably refused to defile themselves with this non-kosher soup. But after they grew weak from hunger and from the pressures of hard labor, a number of them came to me in the pre-Yom Kipur days of 5702 — late September 1941 — and asked if they might be permitted to eat the soup since their lives would ultimately be endangered if they did not eat it.

In brief: Do we look at the present situation, and presently there is no danger to life? Or do we consider that since their lives will eventually be endangered as a result of malnutrition they may already now eat the non-kosher food so as to prevent the eventual danger to their lives?

Response: Medical experts maintained that it was impossible for a person to survive with the nutrition then available to the Jews. The laborers' lives were certainly in danger; famine is an extremely agonizing, drawn-out way to die. I ruled that they might eat the soup now because of the eventual danger to their lives. The rabbi of Kovno, the *gaon* Rav Avrohom DovBer Kahana-Shapira, concurred with me.

13: *Critically Ill Patients Fasting on Yom Kipur*

Question: On the day before Yom Kipur 5702 — September 30, 1941 — I was called to Dr. Zakharin, the director of the ghetto hospital. When I got there, he told me that the lives of many of his patients in the hospital would be in danger if they fasted on Yom Kipur.

Despite the doctor's warning, those frail Jews insisted that on that holy day they wished to join all of Jewry in fasting and in praying that G-d show mercy on His people and redeem them from the devouring German enemy. They did not doubt the danger fasting posed to their lives. They knew their weakened condition would grow worse, that the nutrition situation in the hospital was extremely poor, and that the food in the hospital, inadequate at all times, would certainly be insufficient to restore their strength after a fast. The 200 grams of bread and the bit of black horse-bone soup they would get could not possibly provide them the energy they needed after the fast. Many would grow sicker.

Nevertheless, they insisted that they were relying on G-d to help them survive the fast. The director wanted me, a rabbi, to explain that Halacha did not allow a fast at such a time. He also told me that not only religious patients who had always worshiped and served G-d wanted to fast, but that even people who in their entire lives had never observed Judaism and had not professed any Jewishness wished to fast together with the other patients and the rest of the Jewish people.

I was stunned. In my heart I said, "Riboinoi-shel-oilom, look down from Your heavens and see Your Jewish people. Even at such a time of turmoil and anguish Your spirit moves them and they believe firmly that the Eternal One of Jewry will never fail them, that the light of Jewry will never be put out. Even in the face of death they are ready to sacrifice their lives to sanctify You and to participate as much as they can in the continuity of the Jewish people by keeping Your commandments with all their heart, with all their soul, and with all their being."

I told Dr. Zakharin that I would first clarify to my own satisfaction that the Halacha did in fact require them not to fast, and then do everything in my power to influence them not to endanger their lives by an unnecessary fast.

Response: Since it was the doctor's opinion that if the patients fasted on Yom Kipur they would be endangering their lives, the Halacha is incontrovertible: they were forbidden to fast.

Consequently I spoke to the patients about the great danger involved if they would fast, explaining the seriousness of the ban they would be transgressing. Not only was there no act of righteousness involved but, on the contrary, it was a very great sin to transgress the Torah's commandment which said, "And he shall live by them," not that one should die as the result of fulfilling the commandments. My words, spoken with deep concern, got through to the patients, and they promised that they would heed the doctor's instructions.

One patient, however, who had always been non-religious, stubbornly insisted on fasting that year and refused to accept my explanation that in his weak condition it was imperative to eat. Regrettably, the man died on the night after Yom Kipur. The other patients told me that he had wept throughout the entire day, apparently confessing all the sins of his life in order to die a repentant Jew.

14: *Sanctioning Unsatisfactory Religious Marriages*

Question: On 12 Tishrey 5702 — October 3, 1941 — a distressing rumor reached the ghetto prisoners: the German murderers had decided that since the number of women in the ghetto was greater than the number of men — as the result of previous *Akzionen* (forays) where heads of families had been butchered and their wives widowed and their children orphaned — all women who were husbandless would be taken to be murdered; only those women whose husbands were living would be left alive. This persistent rumor made many unmarried women anxious to marry in order not to be put to death. They found men willing to marry them, and asked the rabbis to arrange *kidushin* (marriages) in accordance with the law of Moshe and Jewry.

Since the ghetto did not have a *mikveh*[1], the rabbis very seriously pondered whether they might be forbidden to honor the requests of the unfortunate women now standing in the shadow of death, for they might be placing a stumbling-block before the couples, who would violate the very serious transgression of *nida*[2]. For even though such marriages might save them from the sword of Damocles over their heads, nevertheless they would be ensnared by the penalty of *kareth*, to be cut off spiritually from this world and the future world for violating this serious prohibition against living with a man without *mikveh*. Not only would the women be liable for the penalty of *kareth*, but their husbands as well.

---

1. Pool for ritual immersion.
2. Intercourse with a woman who has menstruated and not immersed herself in a *mikveh* after the requisite interval and the necessary preparation is punishable by excision (being cut off) from the Jewish people in this world and in the world of reward. See *Leviticus* 18:19 and 20:21 and Tractate *Nida* in the Babylonian Talmud.

The rumor had no known source. Even if someone had explicitly heard from the accursed murderers that married women would be spared, it would have been meaningless, for we were to the Germans like sheep at the slaughterhouse; none of us could tell them what to do. There was thus no assurance that marriage would help these women. It was quite possible that they and their husbands would be put to death by the Germans.

On the other hand, these terror-filled women were quite likely to go to the Jewish police in the ghetto who had the authority to perform civil marriages which were acceptable to the Germans. Civil marriages would lead to grave complications in Jewish law since the police married any couple that came to them and registered them as man and wife without any investigation into whether the woman had been previously married, whether she had obtained a divorce (*get*) or not, or whether her husband might still be alive. It was also possible that the woman might need *chalitza*[3] or be proscribed from marrying this man for another reason. Despite all these reservations, once the woman was registered civilly as a man's wife it was most likely that they would live together as man and wife.

Thus if the rabbis would not arrange *kidushin* for these unfortunate women many more problems would arise from the civil marriages — many more sexual transgressions would occur leading to the birth of *mamzerim*[4] and of *pegumim*[5].

3. Levirate ceremony deacribed in *Deutronomy* 25 : 7-10.

4. The child of a union prohibited in *Leviticus* 18 for which the penalty listed in *Leviticus* 20 is either death or excision, with the sole exception of *nida*, is called a *mamzer* and is limited by *Deuteronomy* 23 : 3 to marrying another *mamzer* or a convert.

5. The child of a union with a *nida* is called a *pagum* — spiritually deficient. Though no legal restrictions are placed on his marriage, many families avoid marriage with a *pagum*. Other families seek indications of personal spiritual growth before allowing such a marriage.

Might it not be wiser for the rabbis to accede to the requests of the women and to arrange *kidushin* for them? For the rabbis would certainly investigate each instance to make sure that no sexual transgression ensued.

The question boiled down to the following: Should the rabbis refrain form arranging *kidushin* for these women because they would be providing an obstacle for the couples since no *mikveh* was available, or should they not withhold *kidushin*, because by their arranging the *kidushin* the couples would marry in accordance with the Torah of Moses and Jewry rather than civilly which would later lead to very serious problems? I was asked by the rabbi of Kovno, Rav Avrohom DovBer Kahana-Shapira, to examine this problem.

Response: After an extremely exhaustive study of the many complexities of this problem, I concluded that we should arrange *kidushin* for these people. Since there was a risk to the lives of the women if the rabbis would not arrange the marriages, and since it was possible for the observant women to immerse themselves in the river, it was best that the rabbis arrange the *kidushin*. This would be far better than having the couples marry civilly at the Jewish police station, which would lead to great complications.

In all cases, the attending rabbi would have to caution them not to cohabit unless the woman undertook to immerse herself in the river according to Halacha. The rabbi might then perform the *kidushin* for the couple on the assumption that they would act in accord with the Halacha.

The rabbi of Kovno concurred with my conclusion.

15: *A Suka¹ of Boards Stolen from the Germans*

Question: The Russians, during their occupation of Lithuania in 1940, had put up blocks of buildings outside the Kovno suburb of Slobodka to house laborers. When the Germans conquered Lithuania, they turned these buildings, many still incomplete, into ghetto housing for the Jews. With the approach of the Sukos² holiday, ghetto prisoners set up a *suka* in an alleyway between two large buildings in Block C so that even in captivity they could fulfill this mitzva. Hidden from passersby, there was some hope that the accursed Germans would not notice what was going on in the alleyway.

The boards that were used to build the *suka* had been taken from nearby workshops where Jews worked as slave laborers. In order to get a proper fit, it was necessary to shorten a number of the boards. Needless to say, the Jews did not have permission from the Germans to take these boards, and certainly not to cut them down to size. Had they been caught, they would have been put to death. But to fulfill this great mitzva according to Halacha, Jews risked their lives. However, the question was raised: Is it permissible to fulfill the mitzva of *suka* with raw materials that are stolen?

Response: The Germans had not brought in their lumber from Germany. All the wood in their possession had been stolen from Jews, who were involved in every phase of the lumber business in Lithuania. They used to buy whole

---

1. A temporary home built to fulfill *Levicitus* 23:42.
2. The festival of booths: see *Levicitus* 23: 23-44.

forests, and owned the lumber mills that trimmed the logs into boards for export to all parts of the world. When the accursed Germans invaded Lithuania they looted the lumber from either local Jews or local non-Jews. Doubtless when the Germans looted the lumber, the owners gave up hope of it ever being returned. All Jewish owners certainly had given up, because they knew they were slated for annihilation. Consequently, whoever took the lumber from the Germans to make the *suka* took it after it had left the possession of the original owner who had surely forgotten that the lumber ever existed.

I therefore ruled that it was perfectly permissible to take the lumber in the first place. Thank G-d, many Jews in the ghetto fulfilled the mitzva of *suka* according to Halacha.

The Germans never did realize that the Jews they were trampling one moment were fulfilling the commandment of *suka* the next moment. While the Germans carried out their *Estland Akzion,* a Jew known as Reb Zalman der Blinder hid in this *suka* and was saved. The Germans looked through all the barracks, but did not look for Jews inside the *suka*.

16: *Pre-Dawn Donning of Tefilin[1] and Praying*

Question: In the days of the anguish that descended upon and devastated the Jews of Lithuania, when the sadistic German government determined to annihilate all of Jewry through horrible decrees of poverty, suffering, pain and — above all, decrees of forced labor that racked the body and depressed the soul — the following problem was posed to me on 22 Tishrey 5702 — October 13, 1941.

At that time, the ghetto prisoners were forced to labor in the airfield next to Kovno, to enlarge it to meet the needs of the German occupation forces so that it could serve as a base for large airplanes and other destructive weapons. The ghetto Jews had to provide 1,000 laborers daily. Work began at 4 a.m. and lasted till after dark. Only after completing their labor were the unfortunate Jews permitted to return home. They had to arrive exactly on time; the slightest lateness resulted in harsh beatings and the risk of death.

I was asked if there was any way the laborers could fulfill the mitzva of donning *tefilin*, for it was impossible for them to fulfill this mitzva during the daylight hours, since at that time they were occupied with the forced German labor. And the Germans surpervising them allowed them no rest, not even for an instant. Anyone suspected of slowing down, of not working competently, was in danger of being killed. The only opportunity the Jews had for fulfilling this mitzva was

---

1. *Tefilin*, phylacteries, are worn on one's head and arm in fulfilment of *Exodus* 13: 9 and 16, and *Deuteronomy* 6: 8 and 11: 18.

30

before appearing for work; in other words, when it was still dark. The question was then, "Might a man don *tefilin* before daylight prior to going to work? And what should he do about reciting *Shema²* and praying?"

Response: Since the workers had no opportunity to don *tefilin* by day, I ruled that they were allowed to don them and recite the blessing at night.

The second part of the question, with its reference to the recital of *Shema* and praying *Shemoneh Essrey³*, I resolved as follows: In our situation, where it was impossible for the unfortunate laborers to pray during the course of the day because their German oppressors did not allow them any respite, it was certainly correct to rule that they might pray before going out to work, even before dawn. Insofar as reading *Shema* is concerned, let them read at least the first verse while they are working, if that is at all possible. If they have the opportunity to read the entire *Shema* and to recite the *Shemoneh Essrey* prayer while working, that is even better yet.

2. *Deuteronomy* 6: 4-9 plus 11: 13-21, read twice daily in fulfilment of **verses 6:** 7 and 11: 19

3. The core prayer (18 blessings) of the Jewish prayerbook.

17: *Making up Lost Prayers*

Question: On the Sunday of *Parshas Noach* 5702 — October 19, 1941 — the Gestapo soldiers demanded from the Jewish Labor Office — whose task was to provide Jewish slave laborers for the Germans — 15 Jews who they said were needed for light work. There was no need for the workers to be young and strong, they could even be old and weak.

On Sundays, the Jewish Labor Office normally sent out those who had worked all week inside the ghetto, giving the 1,000 men who were compelled to work at the airfield a chance to rest. The men who worked within the ghetto walls were pleased to go out to the airfield on Sunday, knowing that they were easing the load of some of their oppressed brothers.

The 15 elderly workers the Labor Office supplied to the Germans that Sunday went out in good spirits, having been told that the work load would be light. But as soon as they stepped outside the ghetto walls, the Germans fell upon them like wild animals, forcing the old people to run and beating them if they slowed down. The work for that day was to clean the Gestapo toilets — without any equipment at all. Locked in the latrines all day without food or water to drink, they were compelled to clean out the German toilets with their bare hands.

At the end of the day when the Germans returned the 15 Jews, it was totally dark. Those broken people, who had suffered so bitterly all day, stepped inside the home of Gapanovitch the tailor on number 15 Vitena Street to pray

1. Night prayer

32

and to attend a Torah class. Despite the fact that he lived in a tiny little room with his wife and daughter, the tailor had made his room available for daily prayers and classes in *Ein Yaakov, Mishnayos, and Chayey Odom*[2].

When I came to teach my class, Gapanovitch — may G-d avenge him — told me that the workers who had just come in to pray were deeply depressed because they had had no opportunity to pray at all that day, having been subjected to cleaning latrines where prayer is forbidden. They had not even had an opportunity to recite the blessings on the Torah that are recited each morning. To the Maariv prayer they knew they could add an additional Shemoneh Esrey[3] to make up for the Mincha[4] prayer. But what could they do about the *birchos haTorah*[5] that they had lost out on?

Response: I instructed them that during the *Ahavas Olom* prayer at the beginning of Maariv they should have in mind the blessing on the Torah. Immediately after the prayers they would have the opportunity to study Torah by joining our regular study group. This solution pleased and consoled them.

2. Classic Jewish works
3. The core prayer (18 blessings) of the Jewish prayerbook.
4. The afternoon prayer
5. The blessings on studying Torah.

18: *Committing Suicide in Order to Be Buried Among Jews*

Question: On 6 Marcheshvan 5702 — October 27, 1941 — two days before the horrifying Black Day of the Kovno Ghetto — when some 10,000 men, women, and children were taken away to be butchered — every one of the ghetto dwellers saw his bitter end coming. At that time of confusion, one of the respected members of the community came to me with tears on his cheeks and posed a question of life and death. He felt that he could not bear to see his wife, children, and grandchildren put to death before his very eyes. For the German sadists had a system for extermination. In order for the murderers to enjoy the suffering of their victims, they would kill the children before the eyes of their parents and the women before the eyes of their husbands as a matter of course. Only after satisfying their bloodlust in this sadistic fashion, would they put an end to the suffering of the heads of the families. Because he felt certain that it would kill him to witness the horrible suffering of his loved ones, he asked whether he might terminate his own life earlier so as to avoid witnessing the deaths of his loved ones. Besides being spared a horrible death of great suffering at the hands of the accursed murderers, he would also gain burial among Jews in the Jewish cemetery in the ghetto.

Response: Although the man knew he would definitely be subjected to unbearable suffering by the abominable murderers, and so hoped to be buried among Jews, he still was not allowed to commit suicide.

Moreover, permitting suicide in such a case meant surrendering to the abominable enemy. For the Germans

34

often remarked to the Jews, "Why don't you commit suicide as the Jews of Berlin did?" Suicide was viewed as a great desecration of G-d, for it showed that a person had no trust in G-d's capability to save him from the accursed hands of his defilers. The murderers' goal was to bring confusion into the lives of the Jews and to cause them the greatest despondency in order to make annihilating them all the easier.

I cite proudly that in the Kovno Ghetto there were only three instances of suicide by people who grew greatly despondent. The rest of the ghetto dwellers trusted and hoped that G-d would not forsake His People.

19. *The Blessing for Martyrdom*

Question: My eyes run with tears again when I think of the Jews who sanctified G-d at the hands of the evil Germans on the Black Day — as the Jews in the Kovno Ghetto labeled 8 Marcheshvan 5702 — October 29, 1941. On that day men, women, and children — young and old, infants and babes in arms — were butchered by the merciless enemy.

On that day an order was issued by the accursed Germans that every single ghetto dweller, without exception, must appear in the Demokratiaplatz for review by the Germans. Whoever stayed home would be put to death.

It is impossible to describe the fear and terror that seized the Jews of the ghetto, all of us aware that our fate was being determined on that day. The ghetto houses were emptied of their inhabitants as parents took their young children in hand; older children supported their elderly parents, and the weak and the ill were moved by their own families. All of us wept as we marched to the plaza of terror, and crying and wailing split the air. It is impossible to describe the agony. We who did not know what our end would be, were certain it could not be a happy one.

The weather was stormy that day. Both snow and rain descended from the skies as if the angels felt our terror and were begging G-d to show mercy upon the remnants of Jewry being sent to their slaughter.

Gathered in the plaza were some 30,000 ghetto dwellers, waiting for the appearance of the German murderer Roka, the Gestapo officer in charge of selection. It was up to him to seal the fate of the waiting Jews, one by one.

A Jew named Eliyahu who had fled from Warsaw to Lithuania, thus escaping the German snare, was aware that most of the people waiting in the plaza would be put to death by the following day. He asked me, "What is the precise text of the *berocha[1]* that sanctifiers of G-d must recite before being put to death? Does one say *'asher kideshonu bemitzvosov vetzivonu al kidush HaShem'[2]* or, *'vetzivonu lekadeish es HaShem'?[3]* He wished to know precisely which text to use to fulfill what might turn out to be the last mitzva of his life. Besides he wished to tell as many people as possible what blessing to recite if their turn came to die.

Response: I ruled that the proper blessing was neither of the texts he had mentioned, but the text established by the author of *Shaloh — Sheney Luchos HaBeris —* which is, *"asher kideshonu bemitzvosov vetzivonu lekadeish shemo borabim,"[4]* the very text that I intended to recite.

Reb Eliyahu repeated the text several times, then proceeded to inform other Jews as to its exact phrasing so that they should be prepared when and if their time came to die in sanctification of G-d.

Some time later he told me that the martyred *gaon* Rav Elchonon Wasserman had told his son, Rav Naftoli — G-d, avenge them both! — who was in the Kovno Ghetto at this time, to recite the text of the blessing as established by the *Shaloh*, and he quoted the Chofetz Chayim as the authority for this.

I also heard from the grandson of the Chofetz Chayim, Rabbi Yehoshua Levinson — G-d, avenge him too! — who was with us in the ghetto, that he had heard his grandfather during the First World War say, when bands of marauding murderers led by Petlura, Machno, and others were wandering through Russia, that one should recite the blessing according to the text of *Shaloh*.

1. Blessing.
2. Who hallowed us with His commandments and commanded us about sanctifying the Name.
3. ...and commanded us to sanctify the Name.
4. ...and commanded us to sanctify His name publicly.

20: *Taking the Property of the Dead*

Question: On 8-10 Marcheshvan 5702 — October 29-31, 1941 — an *Akzion* took place in which some 10,000 men, women, and children were taken away to be butchered. Each of us thought that this might be his last day of life. During this time of torment, one of the respected householders of the city came to me with tears of anguish on his face. He was broken and bitter at the tragedy of his family starving before his very eyes. His children were literally begging for bread, and he had none. A possible solution had presented itself, and he wished to know what to do about it: A family living in the same house had already been totally wiped out in this *Akzion.* Since he knew that the family had no surviving relatives, he wondered whether he might take the little bit of property this family had left in their apartment and sell it in order to raise cash for food for his starving family.

Response: The Halacha was plain: Even if there were living relatives who, according to Torah law, were the rightful heirs of this martyred family, there was no question that they entertained no hope of ever inheriting any of those possessions. Everyone knew that the Germans, after their *Akzionen,* looted everything of value. Whatever they did not consider worth seizing, they left behind. I ruled that the man was free to take the little that was left for his own family. The family of martyrs would certainly be pleased that some of their property had been put to the use of Jews rather than having fallen into the hands of their murderers.

21: *Reusing the Garments of Martyrs*

Question: On the Black Day — 8 Marcheshvan 5702 —
October 29, 1941 — some 10,000 of our brethren were
martyred in the Ninth Fort. Among them was Rabbi
Eliyahu Tchadikov — G-d, avenge him! — who had been a
slave laborer in the Jordan Brigade. He had told me that in
the Ninth Fort there was a storeroom of garments from Jews
the Germans had murdered, and that the pockets of those
garments still contained personal letters, photographs, and
other miscellaneous items which identified the garments as
belonging to the murdered victims. Many of the workers had
found photographs of relatives among the effects: one man
had found a photo of his brother, another had found one of
his mother. The clothes had no bloodstains, proof that the
murderers had stripped their victims before killing them.
Rabbi Tchadikov had asked whether those garments might
be used again, since garments in which people were killed
are forbidden to be worn.

Response: Since those garments had been removed before
the victims were killed, they might be worn not only by the
victims' heirs, but also by any other survivors as well. The
martyred souls would unquestionably derive spiritual
satisfaction in the world of the souls from the fact that their
suffering captive brethren were garbed in warm garments
that had once belonged to them. May the G-d of vengeance
avenge Himself against the evildoers who oppressed His
people, tortured His righteous ones, and murdered His pure
ones!

22: *Reciting the HaGomel Blessing*

Question: On the tragic 8th of Marcheshvan 5702 — October 29, 1941 — a major *Akzion* took place. More than 10,000 people were taken away to be butchered — young and old, men, women, and children. Almost all of them suffered weird forms of death after being tortured physically and psychologically by their merciless butchers.

Some of the miserable survivors of the *Akzion* asked me on the 13th of the month whether they were obligated to recite the *HaGomel* blessing for G-d's mercy in allowing them to survive the purge. On the one hand they had survived an *Akzion* and owed G-d a debt of gratitude; yet on the other hand they were still not out of the Germans' hands; they were still imprisoned within the ghetto walls which were surrounded by an electrified barbed wire fence with armed guards standing ready to utilize their machine guns on anyone who got too close to the barbed wire. Do we regard these survivors as not yet having been released form their troubles, in which case they certainly have no obligation to recite the *HaGomel* blessing? Or do we say that since they were saved from definite death at the same time that thousands were put to death, they are obligated to recite the *HaGomel* blessing?

Response: There was no obligation for the survivors to recite the *HaGomel* blessing since they were still in danger of being murdered. The very fact that they were living inside the ghetto walls indicated the great danger they were in, for who knew what the Germans might yet do! It was entirely possible that the cruel murderers were already then determined to butcher all the survivors. The fact that they were momentarily leaving them alone meant nothing because it was the habit of those diabolical murderers to eliminate the Jews piecemeal. Part of their plan was clearly to confuse the Jews, to delude them with false hopes, and thus lead them into even greater despondency.

Even people who managed to survive a number of such *Akzionen*, so long as they were still imprisoned within the ghettto walls and had not yet been liberated, were not to recite this blessing.

23: *Saying Kaddish[1] for Martyrs*

Question: On 11 Marcheshvan, the third day after the Black Day on which more than 10,000 Jews — men, women and children — were butchered in the Ninth Fort after first being tortured with savage cruelty, a boy who had escaped death crept back to the ghetto and related the details of the savage butchery: The accursed Germans had ordered the doomed Jews to undress at the sides of ditches prepared in advance, and forced them to leap into the pits one on top of the other. Then they had pitilessly gunned them down with machine guns. When the terror of the bullets ended, the blood-soaked ditches were covered with earth, and the living were buried together with the dead. Since many of the Jews had only been wounded, they were still breathing when they were buried alive.

No house in the ghetto was untouched by this massacre. One mourned a parent, another mourned his wife; one mourned his children, another the husband of her youth.

Reb Leizer, the director of the Chevras Ein Yaakov at the Halvoyas Hameis Kloiz, asked if it was imperative to mourn and say *kaddish* for these martyrs.

Response: Rabbi Yaakov Haleivi of Moulin writes in his responsa that even though martyrs attain so sanctifed a level that no one can approach them in spirituality, nevertheless they should be mourned. "I heard from my

---

1. A prayer for the dead recited during public prayer sessions.

teachers that once, after a pogrom in Prague, the question was discussed whether or not to mourn the martyrs. Ultimately, they ruled that they should be mourned."

I therefore ruled that the martyrs of the Ninth Fort should be mourned and *kaddish* said for them. It was a heartbreaking sight to see the survivors in the ghetto rise up together and recite *kaddish* in unison for the loved ones who had been torn from them. May the Healer of broken hearts heal our suffering and bring relief to His people.

24: *Circumcision by an Irreligious Jew*

Question: A Kovno family had assimilated among the non-Jews. There was nothing in their behavior to distinguish them from the gentiles. Moreover they did not even keep the covenant of our forefather Avraham, and had never circumcised their son. In 1941, when the cruel enemy decreed that all surviving Jews must leave the city of Kovno and be sealed off within the ghetto set up in the town of Slobodka, this family was taken along with the rest of the Jews like sheep to the slaughter. All their assimilation was to no avail. The head of the family was cruelly murdered by the accursed Germans, and his wife and children were compelled to suffer exactly what all the other Jews suffered inside the ghetto walls.

The members of this family naturally asked themselves, "Why must we suffer?" They looked upon themselves as gentiles and could not perceive that the accursed evildoers regarded all Jews equally as vermin to be annihilated. Ultimately their uncircumcised son developed a sense of kinship and love for his unfortunate brethren, and he sought a way of rejoining the Jewish people. In his own mind it boiled down to the idea that, "If in death I will not be separated from my people why should I be separated from them in life?" He firmly determined to have himself circumcised in accordance with Halacha.

But there was no G-d-fearing *mohel* in the ghetto who could circumcise this 27-year-old man. A Jewish surgeon, a man who desecrated Shaboss (the Sabbath) publicly, was willing to perform the circumcision. So I was asked if Halacha allowed the doctor to circumcise the young man.

44

Response: According to Halacha one should not restrain a desecrator of the Sabbath from circumcising when there is no other *mohel* in the city or under other pressing circumstances.

In our case one could certainly allow the doctor to circumcise the young man, for there was no more pressing time than one where Jews were being taken out every day to be murdered by the accursed butchers.

1942
to
1944

Holocaust

25: *Reading of Shema[1] by Slave Laborers*

Question: During the winter months, the labor in the airfield began when it was still dark, long before the proper time for reading *Shema*, and ended very late at night.

I was asked how the laborers should fulfill the mitzva of reading the morning *Shema*. During work itself, it was impossible for them to concentrate and read the entire *Shema* properly, since the Germans constantly approached them with work orders and commands, compelling the Jewish laborers to interrupt their reading of the *Shema*. They could only read it in fragments. Nor could they wait to read the *Shema* during the lunch break since the break came after midday, when the time for *Shema* was long over.

Response: Since the slave laborers had no other choice, they were to say as much of *Shema* as possible whenever they could and, if interrupted, continue afterwards where they left off. There was no need for them to start over from the beginning, even if the interruption was very long.

Nonetheless, in order to satisfy all halachic opinions, I recommended that if the interruption was long enough to complete the entire *Shema* in sequence, that they repeat the *Shema* when the next opportunity arises or, at the very latest, during the lunch break.

---

1. *Deuteronomy* 6: 4-9 plus 11: 13-21, read twice daily in fulfilment of verses 6: 7 and 11: 19

49

26: *Electric Lights as Shaboss Candles*

Question: In 5702 (1942), I was asked by the people in the Kovno ghetto whether they might fulfill the mitzva of lighting Shaboss (Sabbath) candles by using electric lights, and whether they might recite the blessing *Lehadlik neir shel Shaboss* on those lights. People who all their lives had been careful to fulfill this mitzva were unable to obtain candles because of the very fact that they were locked up in the ghetto. Electricity, however, was available.

Response: I ruled that where it is impossible under any circumstances to obtain Shaboss candles, it is permissible to recite the blessing on electric lighting. Similarly, one may recite the blessing *Borey meorey hoeish* on an electric bulb upon the termination of Shaboss.

27: *Eating Soaked Matza[1] to Fulfill the Passover Mitzva*

Question: In the winter of 5702 (1942), several months before Passover, many of the Jews in the Kovno Ghetto began to try to figure out ways to fulfill the mitzva of eating matza on Pessach. At that time even the most basic foods were not available in the ghetto, let alone white flour from which matza is normally baked. The ghetto prisoners ate whatever they could get their hands on because the black bread that was rationed out was never enough to keep away hunger, and the Germans guarded against any food getting into the ghetto.

Precisely because of this plight, people made every effort not to be ensnared by depression or apathy but to retain their spirits and their psychological strength, hoping that the evil forces would ultimately be destroyed and the prisoners set free. Many of the ghetto prisoners perceived that the only means available to them of opposing the will of their accursed German warders was to maintain some form of Torah study, along with keeping the *mitzvos* so that the Jewish character would not be destroyed.

Toward this end, I organized a small secret group of men who undertook to find ways and means of obtaining flour so that they could bake matzos and fulfill, at the very least, the mitzva of eating an olive-sized piece of matza on Passover Eve. One memeber of the group was Moshe Goldkorn — may G-d avenge him — a Polish Jew who had escaped the German murderers and found his way to Lithuania, only to be cast into the Kovno Ghetto along with us. This man

1. Unleavened bread

labored in the Jordan Brigade and came into contact with Lithuanians with whom he could barter goods for flour.

Our next problem was how to get the flour into the ghetto, since the Germans guarded each one of the entrances, and were especially careful that no food, from potatoes to bread, should get in through the gates undetected.

But Goldkorn took it upon himself — literally at the risk of his life — to locate a source for flour, and from time to time to smuggle a small amount into the ghetto. His joy at being granted the merit of making it possible for Jews to fulfill the great mitzva of eating matza was enormous.

The flour was hidden in a secret place guarded very carefully so that no harm would come to it. Bit by bit, Goldkorn smuggled in enough flour to bake matzos for nearly 100 Jews, each of whom would receive one olive-sized piece of matza. As Pessach drew nearer, the members of this group, at the risk of their lives, managed to bake the matzos in Block C, *die Kleine Werkstaten*[2], where bread was baked for the ghetto families. With permission from the directors of the *Werkstaten*, this group managed to bake all the matzos over a 10-day period after preparing the oven according to Halacha.

But the happiest of them all was Goldkorn, for he had merited the privilege of bringing the flour in, not only for himself, but for the other Jews. At that time, it was indeed a very great mitzva that Goldkorn had fulfilled — providing the means for so many people to fulfill this aspect of the holiday of freedom in accordance with Halacha, inspiring hope in his fellow-Jews that they might yet live to celebrate this holiday with joy after the defeat of their German enemies.

Two days before Passover, Goldkorn was returning from his labor in the evening. He was stopped by German police and searched. A small bag of flour was found on his person. When the Germans realized that a Jew, despite their strict orders to bring no food into the ghetto, had dared violate their edict, they beat him violently and viciously all along

2. The small workshops.

his entire body, but the worst of it was that they broke all of his teeth. Yet this Jew, throughout all of his suffering, accepted it with love for his Creator, knowing that he had made it possible for so many others to fulfill a precious mitzva.

Afterward, Goldkorn came to me with a very serious problem. As he spoke, he broke into tears. "With my broken teeth, how can I fulfill the mitzva of eating an olive-sized piece of matza? Since I come from a chassidic family, whose custom is never to eat matza that is soaked (*gebroktz*) on Pessach, how can I break that custom now? Is there any way for me to fulfill the mitzva of eating matza?"

Response: The tradition of not soaking matza is a stringency. Halacha does not forbid soaking matza. I allowed the questioner to soak the matza in water even though he was descended from chassidim whose custom was not to eat soaked matza on Pessach — because he had no other way of fulfilling the mitzva, a mitzva for which he had risked his life. I did however instruct him to obtain permission from a *beis din*[3] of three people which would annul the implicit vow of the tradition of his forbears that he had upheld all his life not to eat soaked matza on Pessach.

After we set up a *beis din* which annulled his "vow," he proceeded to fulfill the mitzva of eating an olive's bulk of matza together with all the others who, thanks to him, fulfilled this mitzva. Although his whole body was aching and scarred from the vicious beating the German animals had inflicted upon him, there was no end to his joy and his thanks to G d for granting him the privilege of eating matza despite his wounds and his broken teeth.

3. Jewish court

28: *Unsalted Meat and Bloody Carrion*

Question: In 5702 (1942) the ghetto prisoners managed to obtain a cow and to slaughter it in accord with Halacha. The *shochet* was Reb Tzvi Goldberg — may G-d avenge his death — who had been a *shochet* in Kovno. We did not know whether the accursed Germans really knew that the animal had been smuggled into the ghetto and deliberately ignored the matter, or whether they really had been fooled. They might very well have ignored the matter in order to mislead the imprisoned Jews into thinking that there was still hope and that they might continue to live their miserable lives in "normal" ghetto fashion, just as they had deceived Jews in other places by pretending to be nice to them so that the Jews might be more easily annihilated.

Since salt was extremely expensive — it was almost impossible to obtain any salt with which to salt the meat in accordance with Torah law — I was asked by many of the ghetto prisoners whether there was some way of allowing them to cook the meat without salting it, for otherwise they had no way of enjoying the meat. The meat was vital to them for, from the time they had been imprisoned in the ghetto, they had had no other foods than the miserable rations the Germans distributed from time to time. Since many of the ghetto prisoners were ill or aged and emaciated, this was an opportunity to revitalize their dried-out bodies by eating some meat broth. They were not satisfied with the option of broiling the meat over a fire, because they would then be unable to refresh themselves with the broth. They therefore sought some way for me to allow them to cook the meat.

A second problem raised at that time concerned the rations of non-kosher meat which the Germans distributed to the ghetto prisoners in ½-pound lots per head. Even though it was impossible not to eat this carrion (*neveila*) because of the risk to life that not eating it entailed — for without it the ghetto prisoners would not have been able to survive — the Torah nevertheless prohibits eating blood. Since it was next to impossible to obtain salt to remove the blood from this meat, was there some way to avoid transgressing the prohibition against eating blood?

Response: I instructed the people to boil up water in a pot and then to put the meat in — one small piece at a time — so that there would always be at least 60 times as much liquid in the pot as might get cooked out of the meat. For every half-pound of meat they were to use at least six cups of water. I allowed this solely for those who could obtain no salt at all.

But those people who could obtain salt were not permitted to rely on the above procedure. They were obligated to salt the meat in accordance with Torah law as maintained by Jewry generation after generation. Only afterwards were they allowed to cook it and eat it.

The same was true for the meat rations the accursed Germans distributed to the ghetto prisoners. Those who were able to obtain salt had no right to use this non-kosher meat without salting it first. Even though the danger to life inherent in not eating was great enough to allow them to eat this carrrion, nevertheless whatever could be done to minimize the prohibitions involved in eating it had to be done. Whoever could remove the blood was obligated to do so and thus avoid transgressing the serious prohibition against eating blood.

I was not concerned that people might get the impression that salting carrion made it kosher, for everyone knew that the only reason the carrion was being eaten was in order to survive.

29: *Redeeming a Firstborn Son on Behalf of the Father*

Question: When we were captives in the Kovno ghetto, one of the respected citizens of the community came to me on 25 Teves 5702 — January 14, 1942 — with a heartrending request: His only daughter had become pregnant out of wedlock and had borne a son. The seducer had disappeared; it was entirely possible that he had been captured by the Germans. The man wished to know the Halacha about redeeming his daughter's firstborn son: May anyone who so wishes perform the redemption on behalf of the absent father? Must one consider that if the father were present, he would probably not redeem the baby because he wold be too embarrased to admit that he was the father? The woman's father also wished to clarify whether the person doing the redeeming would be allowed to day the *Shehecheyanu* blessing that is normally recited by the baby's father at the redemption ceremony.

Response: Since most of the people who managed to escape from the ghetto were caught and murdered by the Germans, we assumed that the father was dead. Therefore the obligation to redeem the son fell on the *beis din*, the local communal court.

Even if the father were still alive, any other Jew might redeem the child if he put up the money himself, because we assume that it is the father's wish to have his son redeemed. Even though if he were present the father might not consent to redeem the child so as not to embarrass himself publicly, nevertheless when others do the redeeming he is doubtless satisfied to have his son redeemed.

56

Regarding the blessing, whoever does the redeeming need only recite the blessing, *Al Pidyon HaBein*; he need not say *Shehecheyanu.* But if there were some way to obtain a fresh fruit of the new season or a new garment upon which to recite the *Shehecheyanu* blessing while bearing in mind the redemption of the boy, that would be preferable.

30: *Learning Torah with Nazi Murderers*

Question: On the first of Adar 5702 — February 18, 1942 — the accursed murderers ordered the Jews of the ghetto to hand over all the books they owned, whether sacred works or secular books. They all had to be presented at a central book warehouse which was under the aegis of the "German expert on Jewish matters," the notorious Jewhater, Alfred Rosenberg. A special agent from Rosenberg's staff, Dr. Benkhard, was sent to Kovno to carry out this order.

Since I was in charge of the ghetto storehouse, Dr. Benkhard, together with the commandant of the ghetto, Jordan — may his name be obliterated — demanded that I provide them with a copy of the Talmud, for they wished to know what is written there. They also asked Rabbi Abraham Gerstein — G-d, avenge his death! — to read and translate for them the first page of the volume of Talmud that I provided, which happened to be Tractate *Zevachim*. He asked me if it was permissible for him to fulfill the request of the Germans and teach them Torah. Though he might have been able to talk his way out of doing this, he could only have done so with great difficulty.

Response: In *Midrash Eicha Raba* (3:41) we read:

A Jew passed [the Roman Emperor] Hadrian and greeted him.

"Who are you?" asked the Emperor.

"A Jew."

"Does a Jew dare pass the Emperor and greet him? Hang him!"

A second Jew, upon seeing this, refrained from greeting the Emperor. When the Emperor noticed, he said, "What! The Emperor passes and you do not greet him? Hang him!"

His councillors asked Hadrian, "We do not understand what you are doing. One man greets you and you kill him, and another man who does not greet you, you also kill?"

"Are you trying to teach me how to get rid of my enemies?"

The evil Germans, like Hadrian, treated the unfortunate Jews as they saw fit: When they wished to they butchered them, and when they wished to they shot them or burned them to death. It was therefore extremely dangerous to refuse any wish of theirs. In our situation, it was permissible to teach them the Written Torah if they requested it, and even the Oral Torah, which all authorities hold may normally not be taught to a non-Jew.

I was asked by the evildoers to explain to them the handwritten glosses of Rabeinu Yitzchok Elchonon Spector, the rabbi of Kovno from the 1870's through the 1890's, on the margins of his personal set of Talmud. They also asked me to read and explain to them a responsum written by this great teacher and genius which was bound together with the Tractate *Zevachim* in his *Shas,* and also to read to them from the Torah scrolls in the warehouse. Because of the danger, I was compelled to fulfill their request.

31: *Fulfilling the Mitzva of a Purim Meal with Soup*

Question: Even during the days of terror, the ghetto Jews attempted to keep their spirits up, particularly during the Jewish holy days. On the Purim of 5702 — March 3, 1942 — the Jews were preparing to keep the holiday, insofar as circumstances allowed, in accordance with the Halacha. Nevertheless, the cursed Germans burst into the ghetto in a murderous rage, screeching and screaming that this Jewish day of festivity would be turned into a day of mourning and anguish.

Usually, each day would find 1,000 ghetto inhabitants being forcibly led off to work in a number of locations, but the majority went to the airfield outside Kovno, where the work was more difficult and the workers were hounded and taunted by their overseers more than at any of the other locations.

As soon as the 1,000 laborers had gone early in the morning, the rest of the ghetto, with each passing hour, would breathe easier. Once the Germans had filled their quota of slave laborers, those remaining inside dropped their guard.

But on this Purim the Jews found their hopes for a bit of festiveness dashed when the Germans burst into the ghetto some three hours after the forced laborers had been taken off to work and, screeching and howling, began to grab Jews off the streets and out of the houses, lashing out blows and hurling curses. They proceeded to lead the rest of the remaining ghetto population to some form of slave labor to deliberately disturb the holiday of Purim and to demonstrate once again that there was no hope for Jews. I, too, was taken by the accursed evildoers with the rest of my brethren and forced to work until late at night. Toward nighfall, when we were given a few moments to eat, we hoped to fulfill the mitzva of eating the Purim meal. But to our dismay the only food rationed out was *jusnek*, black horse-bone soup, without even a crumb of bread. My fellow-workers asked me if by eating this black soup they could somehow fulfill the mitzva of eating a festive Purim meal. What we wanted ultimately was a festive commemoration of Purim to spite the German evildoers who had deliberately sought to disrupt our joy.

Response: I told my fellow slave-laborers that they could fulfill the mitzva of eating a meal on Purim with this black soup. Even those halachic authorites who maintain that one should eat bread at the Purim meal require it only where bread is available, but where there is no possibility of obtaining bread, those authorites maintain that one can satisfy the requirement without bread. When I told this to my fellow-Jews their eyes lit up, because I had thus granted them the opportunity to somehow fulfill the rabbinic commandment of eating a meal on Purim as in the past, and their hearts filled with hope that they would yet merit to see the downfall of their evil oppressors.

32: *The Crushed Kohein*[1]

Question: In 5702 (1942) I was asked by the martyr Reb Yechiel son of Mayer Hakohein who used to pray in the Abba Yechezkel Kloiz in Slobodka: The enemy forbade Jewish workers, upon returning from their forced labor, to bring back into the ghetto any food they might have saved from the meager rations doled out to them by the accursed evildoers. The reason behind this madness was not only to prevent the slave laborers from saving a part of their own rations to feed their households — their wives and children — but also to inflict greater anguish upon these helpless men by compelling them to witness the starving of their families.

One martyr, no longer able to bear his children's suffering, hid a piece of bread between his thighs, hoping to sneak it past the accursed enemy. He was caught when the Germans stripped him, tore apart his garments, and made a thorough body search. When they found this bit of dried bread near his testicles, they beat him and kicked him until they had crushed his testicles.

After recovering somewhat from his suffering, this poor Jew poured out his heart to me, "True, the evildoers have prevented me from ever living with my wife again,[2] and I am aware that I can no longer have any children even if I survive. And if I don't survive, if the Germans butcher me, I have faith in G-d that ultimately the butchers will be butchered. Meanwhile, I pray as I've always prayed. But

1. Every descendant of Aaron, the brother of Moses, is a *Kohein* (plural, *Kohanim).*
2. *See Deuteronomy* 23:2.

62

there's one problem. Since I am a *kohein*, I've always been called up to read first from the Torah and now, because of what the Germans did to me, I'm blemished and therefore forbidden to read first. According to Halacha, is there any way I might still be allowed to receive an *aliya*[3] as a *kohein*?

Response: The Torah forbids a man who has had his testicles crushed to live with his wife. But in all other respects, he is a complete Jew. If he is a *kohein* by birth, he is a *kohein* in every respect.

Since this man had always been called up to the first *aliya*, people who see him being called up at the wrong time would wonder what is going on. Had he not suffered enough under the German boot? Did he have to be forced to reveal his shame in public? I ruled that causing him any further suffering was forbidden and that no further limitation or hardship should be imposed upon him.

This unfortunate soul, after I had told him the Halacha, said, "Rebbe, you have revived me! Thank you for putting new life and hope into me, both in this world and and the next world as well, by not cutting me off from my sanctity as a *kohein*, nor impairing my lineage as a descendant of Aharon. And just as you have consoled me, may G-d console you and bless you forever."

3. Lit. "going up" to hear the Torah being read.

33: *Saving Oneself with a Baptismal Certificate*

Question: On the first of Nissan 5702 — March 19, 1942 — I was asked whether a person might purchase a baptismal certificate which — if he could escape into the forest — would enable him to join the partisans.

Response: A baptismal certificate has only one connotation: that the owner of the certificate has, G-d forbid, forsaken his Creator and denied his people, the people G-d chose as His treasure. It is absolutely forbidden for a Jew to use one even though he believes wholeheartedly in the Rock of Israel and its Redeemer. He is commanded to sanctify G-d. I concluded that there was absolutely no way to allow using a baptismal certificate, even if one expected to save his life with it.

34: *Chametz[1] that Cannot Be Sold Before Passover*

Question: With the approach of the Passover festival in the year 5702 (1942), we Jews prepared for the holiday by studying the laws of Passover as we had always done. I was among the Jews imprisoned within the ghetto walls by a nation that was desecrating everything Jewish while shedding Jewish blood like water and allowing no Jew proper burial.

Studying publicly in Gapinovitch's *beis hamidrosh[2]* on 15 Vitena Street I was asked by the ghetto dwellers how they should deal with selling the *chametz* that they, with great sacrifice, had managed to hide to still the hunger of their children. The problems were two. One: Because there were almost no non-Jews within the ghetto walls, there was simply no one to sell the *chametz* to. Even if a gentile were found within the ghetto, it would be impossible to sell the *chametz* to him because of the dangers involved should the gentile betray the Jews and report the food to the German murderers who would then descend upon the Jews like carnivorous hordes and exact penance for the great "sin" of owning food. Secondly, if the *chametz* were not sold, was there a way of permitting it to be eaten after Passover without transgressing the prohibition against eating *chametz* that was owned by a Jew during Passover?

Response: I ruled that the Sages' ban on *chametz* that remained unsold did not apply to the ghetto circumstances

1. Bread or any other product made from a leavened grain.
2. House of study.

where selling was impossible. I told them that whoever owned any *chametz* should come before a *beis din*[3] of three men and, in accord with Jewish law, declare his ownership of the *chametz* null and void. The ex-owner would then put the *chametz* in a hidden place for the duration of the holiday. After Passover, it would be permissible to eat this *chametz*.

3. Court.

35: *Fulfilling the Mitzva of the Four Cups on Passover in the Ghetto*

Question: During the days of evil and destruction, when we suffered all sorts of psychological and physical anguish at the hands of the German evildoers, each ghetto prisoner knew that he had to do everything possible to maintain his courage and strength, never to give up or grow apathetic. That was why we made every effort to observe the faith of our forefathers despite the dangers to body and soul. We knew that a spirit of sanctity was a guarantee of psychological stability in the face of the enemy.

Studying the laws of Pessach with my Tiferes Bachurim students in the period prior to Passover, I was asked by them how they might fulfill the rabbinical commandment to drink four cups of wine, since no wine was available.

The famine in the ghetto was growing worse from day to day, and the only common drink available was tea sweetened with saccharin. And even that could be obtained only with great difficulty. I was asked if one could fulfill the commandment by drinking four cups of this saccharin-sweetened tea.

Response: I ruled that since in the ghetto sweetened tea was considered a popular drink it was permissible to use it for the four cups. The blessing to be recited was certainly *Shehakol*, but there was still a difference between using wine and using tea. Normally one recites a blessing on each cup of wine; but when another liquid is used, one does not recite a blessing on each cup, but only on the first of the four cups — the *kidush*[1]

---

1. Invocation recited before the meals on the Sabbath and on holidays over a cup of wine.

cup — and again on the third cup which is drunk after Birkas Hamozon[2], after the meal.

In order to inspire Jews with hope that the redemption was not far off, and also to fulfill the requirement of the Halacha, my students made the tea available to as many people as possible. Those who could not get this tea were obligated to recite *kidush* on matza, if available. Since they had to recite the blessing of Hamotzi over the matza as part of their *kidush*, they did not have to say *Borey Pri HoAdama* when they ate their Karpas vegetable, which in the ghetto was either potato or onion. Since both were normally eaten as part of the meal, there was no need to recite a separate *berocha*[3] for them once one had said the blessing of Hamotzi.

2. Series of blessings recited after a meal to thank G-d.
3. Blessing

36: *Passover in the Ghetto*

Question: At the approach of Passover many problems arose in the ghetto concerning *chametz* (leavened food) at a time when hunger was growing from day to day and one could not even find an olive's-bulk of *matza*[1] to eat for the mitzva on the first night of Passover. Two of the problems that came up were:

1. Might one eat the black beans[2] that were part of the ghetto food ration?

2. Some people had managed to find dirty potato peels at their places of work. They wanted to pulverize these potato peels and to mix that powder with the little bit of flour that was available to them, and thus bake matzos for Passover. This combination is normally permissible because vegetable and fruit juices are not leavening agents. But here it was imperative to scrub the filth from these peels before grinding them. Yet washing them with water in order to cleanse them would introduce the water, a leavening agent, into the mix. Was there any way to allow the use of these potato peels?

Response: In the horrifying circumstances under which the Jews in the ghetto were compelled to live, there was no question that they were allowed to eat the beans on Passover provided they put them directly into boiling water. Where it was impossible to put them into boiling water and cook them, they could be eaten anyhow.

---

1. Unleavened bread.

2. Ashkenazic Jews may not eat beans and lentils on Passover by rabbinical edict.

As to the filthy potato peels, the great sage Rabbi Avrohom DovBer Kahana-Shapira ruled that the filth had to be wiped off with a cloth or a rag. Under no circumstances were they to be cleansed with water, because the water would act as a leavening agent on the flour. After cleansing the peels with a garment or rag, they might pulverize them and mix in some flour and bake the mix — even on Passover proper. Before the baking they were to puncture the matza cakes with a fork so that they should not bubble up. The sage, may he rest in peace, gave instructions that the details of this procedure be publicized so that no one should act in any other way.

37: *Contraceptives in the Ghetto*

Question: Anguished by the great suffering the accursed Germans imposed upon us, I have put into writing some of the horrors they inflicted upon us so that future generations will know what the defiling evildoers did to us. They darkened our world about us, locked the ghetto gates around us, and proceeded daily to issue new and strange decrees aimed at annihilating us and eradicating the name Jew from the world.

On 20 Iyar 5702 — May 7, 1942 — the evildoers issued an edict that if a Jewish woman were found pregnant they would kill her. I was asked whether Jewish women in the ghetto might utilize contraceptives to avoid pregnancy and the concomitant risk of death.

Response: I ruled that because there was an absolute danger to their lives if the defiling evildoers should discover them pregnant, women might use contraceptive devices before intercourse.

38: *Performing a Caesarean Section on a Dead Woman*

Question: On 20 Iyar 5702 — May 8, 1942 — the Germans issued the following edict: Every Jewish woman found pregnant will be put to death. That very day a pregnant Jewish woman passed by the ghetto hospital. A German noticed her belly and shot her for violating the German order against reproduction. His bullet penetrated her heart and she fell dead on the spot.

Passersby immediately carried her into the hospital, thinking there might be a chance to save her or the fetus. Since she had clearly been in her last weeks of pregnancy, a Jewish obstetrician was rushed over. He said that if surgery was performed immediately the baby could be saved. Since I had witnessed this shocking murder and was present in the hospital, I was asked if, according to Halacha, it was permissible to perform the caesarean section. Since no one could be sure that the baby was still alive, was there a halachic concern with the desecration of the dead mother? In addition, in the remote possibility that the mother was still alive cutting open her abdomen would kill her.

Response: It was clear to me that when a doctor who knows his medicine rushes to operate minutes after a woman's death, declaring that the baby can be saved, one must listen to him because the issue is saving the life of the baby.

Where saving a life is involved, we are not concerned with the desecration of the dead. In this case the mother would be overjoyed if the desecration of her body meant her baby's life was spared. I therefore ruled that the operation proceed as quickly as possible. "Whoever saves a single Jewish life is credited with saving an entire world."

To our great sorrow, our hopes were shattered. The cruel murderers, with typical mad German punctiliousness for keeping records of the living and dead, came into the hospital to write down the name of the murdered woman in their book of the dead. When they found the baby alive their savage fury was unleashed. One of the Germans grabbed the infant and cracked its skull against the wall of the hospital room. Woe unto the eyes that saw this! Charge this act to these cruel murderers and to their children and to their children's children! Let them be repaid for what they have done to us!

39: *A Man the Germans Beat Deaf and Dumb*

Question: Under the accursed Germans we were nothing more than slaves. Our children were taken from us and killed, leaving us broken and childless. Whatever we had was stolen by a brazen nation that hated the old and took no pity on the young. A yoke of steel was placed around our necks. The soil we had to dig up was like rock. We served our enemy in hunger, in thirst, in cold, and in dirt. We were oppressed, robbed, abandoned by the world. And food — which meant the difference between life and death — was something they made us struggle for every day. We got just enough to keep us alive for another day of slave labor. But beyond all the cruelties, an edict was issued forbidding us to leave our place of work for even a moment in case we might want to look through the garbage heaps for scraps of food.

In the year 5702 (1942), Reb Moshe ben Aryeh, who prayed in the *beis hamidrash*[1] where I taught and prayed, the Abba Yechezkel Kloiz in Slobodka, approached me. The man had been beaten so severely that he had lost his powers of speech and hearing. Even though the savages had cracked his bones, battered his flesh, and left him unconscious, his intelligence had not been impaired at all. Though totally deaf and dumb, he was still able to communicate in writing.

He posed a serious problem, expressing in writing his anguish at the cruelty done to him for having violated the German edict against leaving his place on the workline. He had not been able to look on and watch his fellow-Jews

---

1. House of study.

starving, their flesh turning brown and starting to shrivel and blacken from prolonged hunger. Despite the danger involved, he had left his work place and gone into the fields during the potato harvest to gather some vegetables that might help his fellow oppressed.

But the accursed evildoers had caught him at his "crime" and to serve as a warning to other hungry "criminals," they had beaten him so viciously that he became a deaf mute.

Although he gradually learned to live within this new world of total silence, he was profoundly disturbed that he had been robbed of his ability to pray aloud. Also, since he could not recite a blessing to G-d with his own voice, he was afraid he might not be called up to the Torah any longer. In addition, since a deaf mute cannot be counted in a *minyan*[2], he was worried whether his disability rendered him a deaf mute by halachic definition. He requested that I find a halachic solution that would allow him to be included in a *minyan* and, even more important, that would allow him to be called up to the Torah.

Response: I ruled that he was certainly to be included in a *minyan*. But including him as one of the allotted number of men called up to the Torah seemed to be impossible. To uplift his shattered spirit, I suggested that he be called to the Torah together with the reader and, while the reader recited the blessings, that he concentrate on each word.

When he read my ruling, his eyes lit up and he wrote, "Rabbi, you have revived me. May G-d console you and grant you life!"

2. Quorum of ten.

40: *Reciting Nacheim[1]* in *Grace After the Meal on Tisha BeAv[2]*

Question: Among the many decrees issued by the brutal Germans was one that the ghetto supply a fixed number of slave laborers every day and every night.

On the eve of Tisha BeAv 5702 — July 22,1942 — we were gathered at the home of the Nachumovitch family on 7 Vitena Street to pray Ma'ariv before reading the Scroll of Eicha and mourning the destruction of the Holy Temple. We also bewailed the sacred and holy Jews of Lithuania, its Torah geniuses and its simple and pure Jews who together had been butchered by the accursed evildoers. May G-d recall them all, together with the rest of the world's righteous, and avenge the blood of His servants that was shed.

In the midst of our reciting the *Kinos*, the dirges, the Germans burst in and, with terrifying shouts, grabbed the assembled and rushed us off for compulsory labor, complaining that the *Arbeitsamt* (Labor Office) had not provided enough Jews for the night shift. When they realized that the assembled Jews had been mourning the Jewish destruction, they blasphemed G-d and ridiculed the Jewish people,"What are you crying about? What are you hoping for? There's no hope for you! You are never going to be saved from our hands!" They beat us and chased us out of the house, driving all the assembled, young and old, to the airfield.

1. Special prayer recited only on the Ninth of Av.

2. The ninth day of the Jewish calender month Av, upon which the Holy Temple was destroyed twice — in 3338 (422 B.C.E.) and in 3828 (68 C.E.).

There they forced us to slave throughout the night without even a single moment of respite from the intense work. Privately, each of us continued to grieve bitterly at the fate of the Jewish people subjected to so implacable an enemy.

The work was so hard that we could only hope that with the coming of daylight we would be replaced by the laborers of the day shift. But our hope was dashed when the accursed Germans did not allow us to return to the ghetto, and forced us to work through the day as well. Those who did not have strength suffered horribly cruel beatings at the hands of the Germans. They kept us working throughout the day into the following night, without a moment's rest. As the day progressed and the labor did not stop, many Jews fell unconscious to the ground despite the beatings of the German taskmasters to keep them working.

The ceaseless labor and the beatings made it impossible to fast that Tisha BeAv. Thus, when the Germans gave out bits of bread with the black soup called *jusnek*, I instructed everyone to eat without regard for the fast day. I was then asked if one was obligated to say the *Nacheim* prayer when they recited he *Birchas Hamozon* blessings after the meal.

Response: Since most of the codifiers agree that *Nacheim* should be said whenever a meal is eaten on Tisha BeAv, I ruled that the slave laborers should say *Nacheim* when they recited the blessings after their meal.

41: *Risking One's Life to Study Torah or to Pray*

Question: On 13 Elul 5702 — August 26, 1942 — the German enemy issued an edict forbidding the Jews of the ghetto to gather in synagogues or in study halls. The broken-hearted residents, their bodies bent and wracked from long days of slave labor, would forget some of their suffering when they assembled in the synagogues at fixed hours for the study of Torah. Listening to the encouraging words of the rabbis who were enduring the same tortured labor instilled in them a drop of hope in the Holy One of Jewry, Who would ultimately avenge the shedding of His servants' blood.

Despite the German decree, I taught in the *beis hamidrash*[1] known as Abba Yechezkel's Kloiz[2] in Slobodka. When the evildoers turned this house of study into a prison, I moved my group into the Halvoyas Hameis Kloiz, and then into the synagogue in Gapinovitch's house on Vitena Street, and then into the Chayim Shafir Synagogue on Vorena Street next to the Eltestenrat. I devoted my time to daily lectures I gave to the Tiferes Bachurim (the educational network we had for youngsters in the ghetto). In each of these synagogues, I strengthened the crushed spirits of our people. I made every effort to teach them to understand that just as one must bless G-d for the good that He gives us, so must one bless G-d for the evil that He unlooses upon us. Instead of yielding to despair, we must wait for G-d's

1. House of study
2. Small synagouge or study hall.

78

assistance, for G-d is good to those who seek Him out and wait for Him.

The accursed evildoers, plotting treachery after treachery, were aware that this well of hope and comfort inside the synagogues gave Jews courage and strength to stand up to their tribulations. It was no surprise when the Germans issued a decree forbidding public prayer and Torah study under the punishment of death.

Reb Naftoli Weintraub, the *gabbai*[3] of the Gapinovitch Shul — may G-d avenge him — asked me whether Torah law obligated him to risk his life to pray with his daily *minyan*[4] and compelled him to risk his life for Torah study?

Response: I did not have the heart to rule that every Jew should risk his life in order to study Torah or pray with a *minyan*. There were few with the purity of thought that could raise them to the level of a Daniel and his comrades, Chananya, Mishoel, and Azarya, who risked their lives to sanctify G-d even when they were not bound to.

On the other hand, how could I forbid anyone to risk his life? All Jews possess holy souls that originate at the highest level Above and, according to the Halacha, each individual must probe the degree of his personal love and awe of G-d to determine his level of service to G-d and his consequent right or duty to make sacrifices. Beyond any doubt, the Master of Justice and mercy guides each person to act with sensitivity.

In fact, the sacred sons of the living G-d acted as they had always done: They continued to study Torah and to pray with their fellow-Jews.

Even on Rosh HaShona of 5703 — September 12 and 13, 1942 — the Jews did not fear that the Germans would hear the powerful blasts of their *shofar* during prayer. Not only did the Jews gather in the many houses of prayer set up for the holiday, but in the ghetto hospital the assimilationist

3. Official in charge.

4. Quorum

doctors themselves defied the German decree and risked their lives in order to pray publicly.

I, too, despite the decrees, continued to hold regular daily classes in public. When the students at Tiferes Bachurim repaired Mr. Singer's building on 8 Kaklo Street, they built a hideaway with electricity. Upon completion of the job, they even held a dedication ceremony.

Our Torah-study and prayers apparently found favor in the eyes of G-d and we were privileged to survive the enemy.

42: *Abortion in the Ghetto*

Question: On 27 Av 5702 — August 28, 1942 — I was asked whether a woman who had become pregnant in the ghetto might undergo an abortion, because the evildoers and defilers had decreed that any Jewish woman found to be pregnant would be killed.

Response: In that situation, where it was clear that if the Germans discovered her pregnancy neither the woman nor the fetus would survive, I ruled that it was permissible to abort the fetus in order to save the woman's life.

43: *A Castrated Man as a Cantor*

Question: Some two weeks before Rosh Hashana 5703 (1942), when the Jewish prisoners of the Kovno Ghetto were making their plans to blow *shofar[1]* and to pray in unison to G-d for mercy and redemption, the Germans decreed that the Jews were not to hold any public gatherings on pain of death.

Despite the danger, many *minyanim[2]* were organized in the ghetto. Individuals who had never prayed before joined their brothers in prayer. Even Dr. Zakharin, an assimilationist, arranged a *minyan* in the ghetto hospital for Rosh Hashana and Yom Kipur.

At that time the following question arose: It turned out that the man chosen to lead the High Holy Day prayers in the hospital, a Jew with a beautiful voice whose piety and unblemished character met the specific halachic requirements for a prayer leader on such awesome days, had been castrated by the bestial Germans. Did this physical blemish disqualify him from leading the worshipers on the High Holy Days?

Response: For a number of reasons I ruled that he be allowed to lead the prayers: First, because the blemish was not visible; second, the Jews very much wanted him; and last, the arrangement was not a permanent one. I also joined the *minyan* of doctors and nurses who prayed with great devotion in defiance of the German decree.

1. Ram's horn blown on Rosh Hashana.
2. Plural of *minyan*.

82

44: *Cremation to Avoid Burial Among Gentiles*

Question: During the bitter year 5702 (1942) my friend Reb Mordechai Yaffe — may G-d avenge him — came to me with a disturbing problem. He had received a letter from a relative who had escaped to Belgium and found shelter in a village as a Christian. This man's sufferings had brought him to the verge of death, and he was agitated at the thought that when he died his neighbors would bury him among gentiles. How could his body rest in a gentile cemetery? He therefore wrote to Reb Mordechai to find out whether the Halacha allowed for his body to be cremated after death, thus avoiding a gentile burial. Since cremation had grown fashionable, he had no doubt that his neighbors would honor such a last wish.

Response: The Torah requires burial for the dead, but the obligation to fulfill it rests with the relatives of the deceased. The dead person, while still alive, must do nothing to make his burial impossible, such as ordering the cremation of his remains. Should he do so, he causes great anguish to his soul in the world of the spirit for having made it impossible to fulfill a commandment of the Torah.

There is no way cremation can be permitted even if the man's ashes are buried; the very act of cremation constitutes a desecration of the corpse. In addition, cremation removes the possibility of eventual atonement granted to those who are buried. The burial of one's ashes cannot compensate for the cremation in terms of this atonement.

I therefore ruled that the man not dare order his body cremated, but rely on his bountiful Creator Whose mercies extend to all. His hiding of his Jewishness and his living among non-Jews had come about unwillingly, solely out of a desire to save his life. He should therefore not feel guilty about being buried among non-Jews. Ordering his cremation, however, would bring evil upon his soul. Ideally, he should arrange to be buried outside the gentile cemetery and to have his relatives informed of the exact location. That would be the best arrangement. Then perhaps, with the passage of time, when G-d shows mercy to His people and releases them from their troubles, someone might be able to exhume his body and bury it in a Jewish cemetery.

45: *Reciting "Who has not made me a slave,"* *in the Ghetto*

Question: We Jews of the ghetto of Kovno in Lithuania were enslaved by the Germans; were worked to the bone night and day without rest; were starved and were paid nothing. The German enemy decreed our total annihilation. We were completely dispensable. Most would die.

One morning during prayer, Reb Avrohom Yosef, who was leading the congregation in the morning service, reached the blessing, "Who has not made me a slave," and shouted bitterly to the Master of all masters, "How can a I recite the blessing of a free man? How can a hungry slave, constantly abused and demeaned, praise his Creator by uttering 'Who has not made me a slave?' "

Every morning as he led the prayers, he let out the same cry! And many of those who joined him in prayer felt the same way. I was then asked for the Torah ruling on this question: Should the blessing be omitted because it seemed to be a travesty — in which case it would be forbidden to recite it — or was it forbidden to alter or skip any part of the prayer text established by our sages?

Response: One of the earliest commentators on the prayers points out that this blessing was not formulated in order to praise G-d for our physical liberty but rather for our spiritual liberty. I therefore ruled that we might not skip or alter this blessing under any circumstances. On the contrary, despite our physical captivity, we were more obligated than ever to recite the blessing to show our enemies that as a people we were spiritually free.

46: *Opening a Grave to Remove Lost Property*

Question: I was asked by my good friend, Reb Mordechai Yaffe — may G-d avenge him — about a problem linked to the hunger we all suffered. Those who never lived in the ghetto cannot understand our desperation. Life inside the walls deteriorated from day to day. In order to obtain a bit of bread, we sold our garments or other possessions. There was no lack of sellers in the ghetto, but where was one to find a buyer?

The ghetto was sealed. No one could enter or leave without permission from the Germans. All Jews were in the same dilemma. We sought bread and found hunger. We were willing to sell whatever had not yet been looted by the accursed evildoers to non-Jews, but the Germans had forbidden them to enter the ghetto. Violators would forfeit their lives.

Each day, however, the Germans took 1,000 Jews out of the ghetto to work as slave laborers. At night they returned. Outside the walls, some of the laborers occasionally made secret contact with non-Jews.

With the help of these laborers, some jewelry left the ghetto. But because the Germans stripped the Jewish workers on the way out of the ghetto and on their way back, anything larger than a ring or a bracelet could not be spirited out. Only very small items stood a chance of evading German scrutiny, and even that meant risking the bearer's life.

Understandably, the slave laborers acting as middlemen received a share of what they brought back. They truly helped many people survive.

Once a Jew gave another Jew a gem to sell outside the ghetto. After sneaking away from his work area to make contact with a non-Jew, he removed the yellow star worn by ghetto Jews from his sleeve, and walked on the sidewalk. Under German regulations, Jews outside the ghetto were forbidden to set foot on the sidewalks; they were compelled to walk with their German guards in middle of the street to indicate that they were prisoners.

A German soldier recognized him as a Jew and shot him for daring to walk on a sidewalk reserved strictly for Aryans and their friends. After the murder, the dead body was brought back to the ghetto and handed over to the Jews to serve as a warning.

The martyr was buried, as is customary, in the garments he was killed in. Only afterwards, when the owner of the stone demanded his gem from the bereaved family, the gem which could add a few days of life to his starving family, did someone recall that it had been stitched into the martyr's clothes. I was asked if it was permissible to open the martyr's grave in order to return the gem to its owner.

Response: I ruled that it was permissible to open the grave and remove the stone because the owner of the gem was justified in claiming, "Honor the dead man, but return my gem!" In addition, since the owner had requested the return of his gem within three days of the burial, it was not yet considered a desecration of the dead to open the grave. Moreover, there was the consideration of obtaining food and saving lives.

47: *Eating in the Presence of a Corpse*

Question: During the days of terror, the accursed Germans continually restricted our living space. Eventually, the ghetto, which had been inside Slobodka, was transferred to a location outside town where Jews had never lived. There were not enough dwellings for everyone. Each house swarmed with people and grew so crowded that there was barely any room to breathe in.

At that time, one of my friends, Reb Efrayim Mordechai Yaffe — may G-d avenge him — posed the following question. A Jew had died in his room that night. The funeral would take place the next day, but the body would have to remain in the room until the funeral. In this room lived a number of people who would rise before daylight to make their preparations before setting out for their long hours of slave labor. Reb Efrayim's question was whether these people could eat their pre-dawn meal in the same room where the dead man was lying. Because of the great cold, it was impossible for them to eat their meal outside; nor could they forego their breakfast because it was not possible to survive a day of slave labor without food. Might they be allowed to eat in the presence of the corpse?

Response: In that case, where it was impossible for the unfortunates to eat their meal in any place other than the room with the corpse in it, I relied on the authorities who recommend that a screen be put up between the dead body and the diners while they eat. But if that too were impossible, I ruled that they should eat in the presence of the body, for not to eat would endanger their lives.

48: *Kohanim[1] Wearing Shoes While Blessing the People*

Question: In the ghetto we not only suffered hunger and poverty, but lacked the basic garments to keep ourselves warm because they had long ago been shredded into rags. We literally shivered through the winter months.

The greatest problem was the lack of shoes. In order to protect ourselves from frostbite, we used to wrap our feet in any rag we found. Fortunate were those who found some kind of abandoned shoe or boot to stick their ragged feet into and protect them from dampness and frost.

Hygiene in the ghetto was non-existent. There was nothing to clean oneself with. There was no soap. There was a constant shortage of water, and there was certainly no hot water. Because of such unsanitary conditions, every ghetto prisoner suffered from boils. Itching was part of ghetto life.

When the Jewish holidays approached, the following question arose: How should the *kohanim* handle the problem of raising their hands to bless the public? Normally the *kohanim* remove their shoes and bless the public in their bare or stockinged feet. But the filth made it impossible to remove their shoes. For if they unwrapped the foul-smelling rags from their infested feet, the stench rising from the rotting rags would pollute and defile the air. I was asked if it was permissible for the *kohanim* to bless the public without removing their so-called shoes, or was it better for them not to bless the public at all?

1. Every descendant of Aaron, the brother of Moses, is a *Kohein* (plural, *Kohanim*).

Response: In order that this mitzva not be abandoned and forgotten, I ruled that the *kohanim* should bless the public even with their feet in rags and quasi-shoes. It was preferable to have them bless their suffering brethren with love and pray to G-d that He soon terminate their bondage, than to abandon the blessing of the *kohanim*.

49: *Chametz After Passover*

Question: As Passover of 5703 (1943) approached, the Germans sent into the Kovno ghetto the bread ration for the following two weeks to be distributed by the Eltestenrat, the Jewish Community Council or council of elders. I was asked to detail the correct manner of dealing with this *chametz* (leavened food) over the Pessach (Passover) period. Because of the danger to life involved, it was impossible to sell the *chametz* before Pessach to a non-Jew, because the Jews were forbidden to speak to non-Jews or to have any dealings with them, and also because the Jews did not want the non-Jews to know that they had bread.

A second issue was the *halacha* (law) that *chametz* owned by a Jew during Passover may not be eaten by any Jew after Passover. How, if at all, did this law apply to our situation?

Response: In our case there was no reason to be stringent about this bread after Pessach. Under the law of the accursed Germans, everything owned by the Jews belonged to them; they took whatever they wished whenever they wished, and no one could stop them. In this particular case, the bread definitely belonged to them and was given to the Eltestenrat solely for purposes of distribution, not for it to be considered Jewish property. Surely if the Germans had found anyone stealing any of that bread, they would have put him to death.

According to Torah law it is sufficient for a person to simply nullify the *chametz* in his possession, in order for him not to be considered its owner. We do not normally follow this procedure. But under the unusual circumstances of the ghetto, I ruled that if the Jews simply nullified the *chametz* before Pessach, that would remove any vestige of their personal ownership of it. Moreover, even if the Jews did own the *chametz*, since it was impossible for them to sell the *chametz* to a non-Jew, the fine imposed by the Sages on *chametz* not sold before Pessach would not apply to this situation.

50: *Public Prayer with Hidden Participants*

Question: In the midst of the horrors of the Kovno Ghetto, the prisoners found great consolation in the study of Torah, which rejuvenated their spirits. They studied individually and in groups, and created fixed places for their public prayers.

The area that the accursed Germans cordoned off for the ghetto was so small that there was barely enough living space for everyone inside, let alone places that could be used for prayer or Torah study. The Tiferes Bachurim group where I taught young and old suffered from a terrible lack of space. Finally we found an unfinished building at 8 Hakala Street. Although there were no floors, doors, or windows, and the heaps of dirt everywhere made the place uninhabitable, the Tiferes Bachurim boys cleaned out the piles of filth and began to restore the building. After putting in a floor, doors, and windows, they constructed a table, benches, and shelves. They also built an ark for Torah-scrolls, placing it between a window and a hiding-place that they had created in the rear. After electricity was installed, the place was suitable for prayer and Torah study. It was now the *beis hamidrosh[1]* of the Tiferes Bachurim group.

Since this building was close to the ghetto gate, where the Germans would descend to grab people for slave labor, we could hear their shouts and yells when they charged through. The young members would hide in the hideout built behind the ark in case of a sudden search, because the Germans, looking for strength and youth, rarely took the old and weak off to forced labor.

1. House of study.

Rabbi Ephraim Oshry

I was asked by the younger members of the Tiferes Bachurim whether, when they had to hide in middle of a prayer service and were unable to see the others who were praying inside the room, their prayers were considered prayer with a *minyan*[2] or were counted as private, individual prayer.

Response: The very question asked by these young people testifies to what degree the light of Torah and *mitzvos*[3] penetrated the ghetto darkness in those days of fear and terror. How great was their fear of G-d! Not only did they pray, despite the dangers and hardships, but they also sought to fulfill the mitzva of praying with a *minyan*. I ruled that since the boys could hear the others saying *kadish*[4] and *kedusha*[5] while they waited in their hideout for the Germans to pass, they were fulfilling the obligation of praying in public. It is conceivable that if there were fewer than ten men in the *beis hamidrosh* itself, those in the hideout could not be included in the *minyan*. But so long as there were ten others, they were considered as having prayed with the *minyan* if they heard and could participate in what was going on in the *beis hamidrosh*.

2. A quorum.
3. Commandments.
4. A prayer for the dead recited during public prayer sessions.
5. A responsive reading, that is part of the prayer service.

51: *Does a Ghetto Home Need a Mezuza?*

Question: In the days of our imprisonment in the Kovno Ghetto, without any link to the outside world, we ran out of all our mitzva supplies such as *tefilin[1]* and *mezuzos[2]*. A number of people asked me what to do since their *mezuzos* had become invalid and it was impossible to obtain fresh *mezuzos* to replace them. The underlying question they had was whether the ghetto apartments really required *mezuzos*. Since there was no way in or out of the ghetto without permission from the Germans, and the ghetto was surrounded by an electrified barbed wire fence, and machine-gun-armed guards made sure that no one even went near the fence, the dwellers of the ghetto were really no more than prisoners. Does a prison dwelling need a *mezuza* or not?

Response: The ghetto rooms were unbearably overcrowded; beds were almost literally one on top of another. Such rooms could in no way be considered normal, permanent dwelling places, because if a person had the option he would leave them as soon as possible. Those dwellings were beyond any doubt temporary residences, whereas a *mezuza* is required only in a permanent residence. This is why a *suka[3]* requires no *mezuza*.

1. *Tefilin*, phylacteries, are worn on one's head and arm in fulfilment of *Exodus* 13: 9 and 16, and *Deuteronomy* 6: 8 and 11: 18.

2. *Mezuzos* (singular, *mezuza)* are parchment scrolls containing two paragraphs from *Deuteronomy*, 6: 4-9 and 11: 13-21, which are attached to the doorposts of a Jew's home.

3. A temporary home built to fulfill *Leviticus* 23: 42.

Moreover, the accursed Germans took ghetto prisoners out every single day to be killed. No one knew when his turn would come. Every day people bade each other farewell, "Auf Wiedersehn in yenner velt" (See you in the next world"), because they had no idea whether they would ever see each other again alive.

A standard ghetto joke was, "We're really dead men on vacation." That was the degree to which people were not sure of their lives. Clearly the ghetto dwellings were temporary. I therefore ruled that those apartments and rooms did not need *mezuzos*.

On the other hand, if someone owned a *mezuza* and wished to affix it to his doorpost so as to recall G-d's unity, he thereby fulfilled a mitzva, but he was not to recite a *berocha*[4] when he attached the *mezuza* to the doorpost, since according to Halacha the *mezuza* was not required.

4. A blessing.

52: *Tzitzis[1] Made from Stolen German Wool*

Question: In the days when we were locked up in the ghetto, Jacob's voice was still to be heard studying Torah, albeit in secret to protect the scholars from Esau's bloody hands. The Tiferes Bachurim, a group of boys whom I taught, continued to study Torah in unison daily. One member of the group, Meir Abelow — may G-d avenge him — sought ways to make it possible for the students to fulfill the mitzva of *tzitzis.* There were no *tzitzis* available in the ghetto. And, because we were locked into the ghetto, there was no way for us to obtain ready-made *tzitzis* or the fibers to make them from any other place: there was no link between the ghetto-dwellers and Jews living outside the ghetto. Anyone caught communicating with Jews outside the ghetto was put to death immediately.

Abelow had found a way to obtain *tzitzis* for at least the members of our little Tiferes Bachurim group. His plan was as follows: Since he worked in one of the *Werkstaten*[2] where the Jewish slave laborers worked full time, and there was much wool available there, he planned to steal some strands of wool, secrete them, and bring them into the ghetto for the purpose of spinning them for *tzitzis.* His precise questions were:

    1. Is it permissible to fulfill the mitzva with *tzitzis* made from this stolen wool?

    2. How does this affect the person taking the wool?

---

1. *Tzitzis* are the fringes attached to the four cornered garments worn by Jews in fulfilment of *Numbers* 15: 37-41.

2. Workshops.

3. Since it is impossible to obtain any cloth from which to make a garment on which to put the *tzitizis*, may one take a large *tallis*[3] and cut it in two in order to turn it into two small *arba kanfos*[4]? Would this constitute demoting a sanctified object to a lesser degree of sanctity?

The youngsters at Tiferes Bachurim were anxious to fulfill the mitzva of *tzitzis* properly because they did not know what was in store for them. They therefore wished to wear *tzitzis* at all times so that if they were, G-d forbid, taken to be killed they might be buried wearing *tzitzis* in accord with Jewish custom.

Response: I ruled that taking the wool from the Germans did not constitute theft and that the Tiferes Bachurim boys might use the wool for making *tzitzis*. Rebetzin Abelow, Meir's mother, spun the *tzitzis* for all the boys as well as for other Jews. As to the second question, since there was no other way to obtain cloth for four-cornered garments, rather than allow the mitzva of *tzitzis* to go unfulfilled, I relied on the opinion that one may cut a big *taliss* in two, to turn it into two small garments.

This brought great joy to the members of Tiferes Bachurim, who were thus granted the opportunity to fulfill this great mitzva which, according to Scripture, is equivalent to all the *mitzvos* together.

3. A large four-cornered garment, usually worn at prayer.
4. A small four-cornered garment, usually worn either over or under a man's shirt.

53: *Burying a Sabbath Desecrator Among Sabbath Observers*

Question: During the horrors of the holocaust, while we were prisoners in the Kovno Ghetto, the German murderers brought suffering upon the dead as well as upon the living. They decreed that the ghetto Jews themselves must be responsible for their own dead and must bury them in the part of town reserved for sewage and garbage disposal. In addition, they forbade putting tombstones or markers on the graves, allowing only numbers, as if our dead were worse than dogs. Later they revised their regulation to allow the Jews to place wooden markers on the graves.

Even though the burial ground was an insult to any human being, the ghetto Jews consoled themselves with knowing that at least they could still be buried among other Jews.

One day a ghetto prisoner died from cancer. He had suffered greatly because the German defilers refused to allow the ghetto doctors to inject any of the sick with painkillers no matter how dangerously ill they were. I learned that fact from the hospital director, Dr. Zakharin.

The dead man had been a freethinker and a public desecrator of the Sabbath, who had kept his store open each Shaboss and Yom Tov and never attended synagogue. To his credit, we knew that upon being forced into the ghetto he had said, "Now if I die I will be buried among Jews without any segregation." No doubt he was referring to the fact that had he died in Kovno before the Germans invaded Lithuania, the community would not have buried him alongside Sabbath-observant Jews. As to how he had conducted his life within the ghetto, whether he had still

99

desecrated the Sabbath or had come to pray in public, we knew nothing. It was certainly conceivable that in the ghetto he had privately repented before G-d and lived like a proper Jew.

I was asked how to deal with his burial. Was he to be buried like every other Jew on the assumption that he had repented, or were we to take his statement upon arriving in the ghetto as merely an observation and not a sign of true repentance?

Response: Since the man had lost his family to the Germans, had been robbed by them, and then been cast into the ghetto, we took his statement as his confessional recognition of the futility of his efforts to live in emulation of non-Jews. Probably, when he saw the murders of his own son and son-in-law he turned away from the epitome of Western civilization — the evil German nation — and turned back to his G-d and to his people. I therefore ruled that he was to be buried like any other Jew who died in the ghetto; that he be provided with *tachrichim*[1] and that he be treated with the same respect as all observant Jews.

Afterwards it was brought to my attention that the man had done genuine *teshuva*[2]. Witnessess testified that he used to don a *talis*[3] and put on *tefilin*[4] every day at home. Besides, he used to wear a *talis koton*[5] every single day. After his burial, these religious items were found in his room, a sign that he had genuinely repented.

---

1. Shrouds.
2. Penitence.
3 A large four-cornered garment, usually worn at prayer.
4. *Tefilin*, phylacteries, are worn on one's head and arm in fulfilment of *Exodus* 13: 9 and 16, and *Deuteronomy* 6: 8 and 11: 18.
5. Small *talis*

54: *A Man Whose Left Hand the Germans Amputated*

Question: Among the prisoners in the Kovno Ghetto there was a young man from Berlin, about 27 years old. A student of law and biology, he also knew a number of European languages. Prior to his imprisonment, he had been a freethinker who cared nothing for religion, but after entering the ghetto and making contact with Orthodox Jews, he returned whole heartedly to Judaism. He deepened his knowledge of Judaism and became a man of pure faith which showed itself in his thinking and his actions. Weeping when he prayed, he said the words with great *kavonoh*[1] especially his recital of blessings, particularly on *tzitzis*[2] and *tefilin*[3]. Inside the ghetto with us, he learned the spiritual value of these *mitzvos*[4] and their unique importance to the Jewish people. Despite the awful hunger that reigned everywhere, he was extremely cautious with every bit of food that came into his mouth. He ate only bread and potatoes or other vegetables. In addition, he would fast every Monday and Thursday. No wonder he was physically very frail.

Another Jew, concerned about restoring the young man's health, got him taken on as a worker in the kitchen where the food for the slave laborers was prepared. There he could eat somewhat better than in the rest of the ghetto. But not for

---

1. Sincere intent.

2. *Tzitzis* are the fringes attached to the four cornered garments worn by Jews in fulfilment of *Numbers* 15: 37-41

3. *Tefilin,* phylacteries, are worn on one's head and arm in fulfilment of *Exodus* 13: 9 and 16, and *Deuteronomy* 6: 8 and 11: 18.

4. Commandments

long. The kitchen surpervisor was a German known for his evil ways. He accused the young student of stealing potatoes. As a penalty the accursed Germans amputated the young man's left arm to the shoulder, claiming that they really should have amputated both arms but had left him the right one so that he could continue to work while suffering.

No words can describe this young man's anguish, not only because he had been turned into an armless cripple but because now he was prevented from fulfilling the commandment of the Torah to don *tefilin* on the left arm. Weeping bitterly, he came to me and asked whether he could fulfill the mitzva of *tefilin* by donning them, with the help of others, on his right arm.

Response: I ruled that even if someone else put the *tefilin* on his right arm, he would be fulfilling the mitzva. He rejoiced at the ruling and, as he walked out in good spirits, remarked, "The accursed Germans did not succeed in robbing me of the mitzva of *tefilin*."

55: *The Hoarse Kohein*[1]

Question: The labor brigades were units of 20 men who were not part of the 1,000 slave laborers who went out daily to toil in the airfield outside Kovno. These smaller brigades were assigned various tasks that were not as arduous as those of the slave laborers in the airfield. Besides, they were fed better.

Understandably, everyone wanted to work in the smaller brigades, where it was easier to save some of the food from their meals and to smuggle it back into the ghetto for their families.

Among the brigade workers was a man named Moshe, who was the only son of an ailing mother. Sick and hungry, she relied on the extra bits of food that Moshe saved from his daily rations. One day Moshe got caught sneaking a piece of bread back into the ghetto. He had hidden it inside a rag that he tied around his neck like a scarf. However, when the workers returned from their detail to the barbed wire entrance to the ghetto, the German *Jefreiter* Neumann searched Moshe. When he found the bread, he beat him savagely, concentrating on the neck, until Moshe fell to the ground unconscious. Even then, the beating did not stop. Only by G-d's mercy did Moshe remain alive. As a result of the beating, his vocal chords were damaged. From then on, Moshe could not speak in anything louder than a hoarse whisper.

Since Moshe was a *kohein*, he asked me whether he was

1. Every descendant of Aaron, the brother of Moses, is a *Kohein* (plural, *Kohanim).*

103

still allowed to go up to bless the people with *birkas kohanim*[2] despite the injury to his throat.

Response: I ruled that Moshe might go up together with his brother *kohanim* to bless his fellow-Jews. From the day of his beating, he had horrible nightmares in which the enactment of the beating was so vivid that he used to jump out of bed trembling. There was no reason to make him suffer doubly by causing him spiritual anguish over and above his physical suffering; it was enough that the accursed Germans had crippled him for the rest of his life. I therefore decided that it was a great mitzva to encourage this *kohein* to rise up from the kick of the German boot and show himself in public as the equal of his brother *kohanim* by blessing his fellow-Jews with love.

2. The blessing recited by the *kohanim*

56: *Risking One's Life to Join the Partisans*

Question: Every day the Germans would take more than 1,000 people to slave labor on the airfield near Kovno. Whenever they found it difficult to fill that quota, they immediately grew infuriated and swept through the ghetto in a murderous mood to capture additional Jews. This was before they placed the burden of supplying the 1,000 men for each of the two shifts every day on the *Eltestenrat*[1].

When the Germans swept through the ghetto, their faces drained of human semblance, they acted like vicious beasts seeking solely to quench their bloodthirst. They would attack unarmed Jews, beat them mercilessly, and do what they could to denigrate them. In the ghetto, every day was worse than the previous one. Countless new edicts were issued to confuse and frighten Jews. The Jews would ask each other, "What's the latest rumor? What's the latest story? What's new today?"

One day a report spread through the ghetto that the Germans had decided to transfer a large number of people to another camp. We knew that this meant a death camp. On the heels of this rumor came a new one. A large number of ghetto prisoners were planning to escape that night to join the partisan units in the forests that were fighting a guerilla war against the Germans. At least that way they could stand up to the enemy.

The problem, however, was that the road to the forest was extremely dangerous. In addition, the ghetto was surrounded by an electrified barbed wire fence — touching it was suicidal — and watchtowers with machine-gun-armed German sentries who were on duty day and night. If all that

1. Council of Elders.

might not keep the Jews from escaping, a great searchlight lit up the entire area outside the ghetto.

The partisans lacked weapons and, as a rule, they accepted only people who brought their own weapons. This rule increased the risk of escaping from the ghetto. Any Jew found outside the ghetto would immediately be killed by the Germans. But if they caught a Jew with a weapon in his possession, his treatment would be far worse than a quick, simple death.

To add to all these dangers, most partisan groups in the forests had little desire to accept Jews. Antisemites themselves, the partisans were fighting the Germans for their own reasons, and a Jew who fell into their "protective" hands more often than not paid with his life.

In consideration of all these factors, I was asked by Reb Yitzchok Gold whether Halacha permitted a ghetto prisoner to risk escaping into the forest in the hope that G-d would help him stay alive.

There seemed to be two approaches to take: Within the ghetto, the danger to one's life was certain, whereas escaping put new hope into one's life. The standard ghetto joke the prisoners used to express the certainty of death within the ghetto walls was to call the ghetto dwellers, "dead men on vacation." In other words, we looked upon ourselves as dead men whose lives were no more than temporary reprieves. Even during the periods when there were no *Akzionen* (roundups), the lives of the Jews in the ghetto were always in peril. For any little infraction, the Germans would shoot to kill. It made no difference whether the German imagined that the Jew had been disrespectful to him, or whether the Jew had had a crumb of food in his clothing when he came back from slave labor. The ghetto itself constituted an immediate danger to life, whereas life outside was not as absolutely dangerous. Outside the ghetto there was always a vital element of uncertainty: one might survive.

On the other hand, one could make the following evaluation: Life in the ghetto posed no immediate danger. Other rumors had it that those who remained in the ghetto would come to no harm so long as they worked and fulfilled all the German demands, while the the danger to those who escaped to the forest came not only from Germans but also from Lithuanians who either handed such Jews back to the Germans or killed them themselves.

Response: It seemed to me that living in the ghetto was definitely a danger to life. The entire purpose of isolating the Jews and imprisoning them in ghettos was solely to rob them of everything they possessed, to enslave them for their labor value, and then to destroy them physically. On the other hand, escaping to the forest offered the survivor another chance at life. Whoever gathered up the courage and decided to escape did so only after thoroughly investigating and weighing his chances.

From time to time we saw partisans in the ghetto, evidently getting in — and out again — without trouble. Anyone who wished to join them was given instructions as to how to find his way through the forest to the partisan hideouts. Although the paths were risky, the partisans obviously survived. Clearly, the accursed Germans' declaration against the Jews made it obligatory for the Jews to fight back and do to them as they were doing to us.

I therefore ruled that one should not undermine the spirit of those who wished to escape to the forest. Rather, one should encourage and support them, and give them every possible assistance in obtaining weapons and ammunition so that when they arrived they would be ready to fight.

57: *Praying on Tisha BeAv[1] Morning with Talis[2] and Tefilin[3]*

Question: In those days of darkness, the ghetto dwellers were aware that in order not to fall into the snares of despondency and desperation that the Germans had spread, they had to maintain their physical and spiritual courage.

Despite the hunger and suffering, we never gave up our will to live, particularly to live the life of Torah and fulfillment of G-d's commandments. We were determined to stick it out and survive. At the risk of death, every one of us in the ghetto did everything he could to maintain his spiritual life and to keep the holy light of our tradition burning. We spared no effort to fulfill as many of the laws of the Torah and the traditions of our fathers as possible because we knew that fufilling the *mitzvos[3]* was the strongest guarantee that the German enemy would not succeed in annihilating the sacred Jewish people from under G-d's heaven.

During festivals, the accursed Germans made it a habit to taunt us and try to shatter our spirit. On the fast of the Ninth of Av (Tisha BeAv), they made special efforts to upset us. In Responsa number 40 I describe how they dealt with us on Tisha BeAv night in the synagogue — how they beat us and dragged us off for a night shift of slave labor.

At the time of that incident, I was asked the following question: In view of the likelihood that the Germans would

1. The ninth day of the Jewish calender month Av, upon which the Holy Temple was destroyed twice — in 3338 (422 B.C.E.) and in 3828 (68 C. E.)

2. A large four-cornered garment, usually worn at prayer.

3. *Tefilin*, phylacteries, are worn on one's head and arm in fulfilment of *Exodus* 13: 9 and 16, and *Deuteronomy* 6: 8 and 11: 18.

4. Commandments.

return to the ghetto on Tisha BeAv morning to drag more Jews off to slave labor just as they had done during that night, was it permissible to get up early in the morning to pray Shacharis[4] wearing *talis* and *tefilin*, contrary to established Halacha that on Tisha BeAv one does not don them for the Shacharis prayer but waits for the Mincha[5] prayer? They feared that under the cruel boot of the Germans, they would be unable to fulfill the mitzva of donning *talis* and *tefilin* that entire day.

Response: Since there was no opportunity to don *talis* and *tefilin* during the day because of fear of a reprisal *Akzion*, I ruled that one might rely on the codifiers who maintain that on Tisha BeAv one should don *tefilin* and wear a *talis* even at Shacharis. Although we do not normally follow those codifiers, in the face of such evil I ruled that the men might rely on them, especially because their desire to fulfill *mitzvos*[6] in the midst of their troubles was so strong.

4 Morning prayer
5. Afternoon prayer
6. Commandments

58: *May a Jew Write the Letters R.C. (Roman Catholic) in His Passport?*

Question: Among the imprisoned Jews in the Kovno Ghetto were German Jews who had been exiled by the Hitler regime. Among them was a Jew who possessed a German passport issued before the outbreak of the war, and whose name was absolutely not Jewish.

As life for the ghetto prisoners grew more difficult, new decrees appearing daily, this Jew decided to escape, hoping that he would be able to hide among the gentiles, since his appearance and name concealed his Jewish identity. He asked the following question: In order to complete the deception, he would have to write into his passport the two letters "R.C." to show that the bearer of the passport was a Roman Catholic. Thus anyone inspecting his passport would be convinced that he was a gentile by birth. Since adding in these two letters might appear to be admitting or confessing to a deity other than the G-d of the Jews, he wanted to know if that was forbidden or permissible.

Response: I ruled that he might write the two letters R.C. for, even though the non-Jews would think they mean that he is a Roman Catholic, he was free to have in mind the Hebrew meaning of the two letters. It was irrelevant how the non-Jews would construe those letters.

59: *Greeting Fellow-Jews Bareheaded*

Question: Before the Jewish slave laborers were led off to work, the Germans would line them all up for a head count to make sure everyone was present. During the count, which was called *Appel*, the workers were ordered to stand hatless and, as an exercise in further dehumanization, were forbidden to greet the German guards. As a consequence, the workers were extremely cautious during the head count not even to greet their fellow-Jews lest the Germans think that they were greeting one of them.

During my studies with the Tiferes Bachurim group, I explained that all of us shared the responsibility to inspire our fellow-Jews, and that we must never allow the ghetto horrors to drown our spirits. For if, G-d forbid, we grew despondent, the work of the abominable Germans would be made easier. Their underlying purpose was to force us to a point where we would no longer regard ourselves as human — anything to break our faith in the Eternal One of Israel.

One way of spiting the Germans was to keep treating ourselves with respect, making their goal of annihilation all the more difficult. Something as simple as one Jew greeting his fellow-Jew would strengthen our broken spirits and inspire us to keep on living, instead of accepting suffering apathetically.

So we undertook to say "Sholom" whenever we saw each other since it was a word the Germans would not be likely to construe as a greeting since they did not know its meaning.

One of the students, Meir Abelow — may G-d avenge him — asked, "Since *Sholom* is one of the names of G-d, how can we say His name during the *Appel* while standing bareheaded?"

Response: True, "Sholom" is one of G-d's names, but it was permissible to utter it for two reasons. First, Halacha follows the opinion of the mishnaic sage who permits uttering any of the seven divine names when one is bareheaded. The second reason is a doubt whether the name "Sholom" has the same weight as the seven divine names. Therefore, when absolutely necessary, one is permitted to utter the name "Sholom" even while his head is uncovered.

Clearly, the Jews undergoing a head count during *Appel* were not only to be allowed to greet each other with the word "Sholom" despite their bare heads, but even encouraged to do so in order to retain an element of normalcy and inspire each other under those subhuman conditions.

60: *Donning Tefilin[1] before Bar Mitzva[2]*

Question: In the ghetto hell, we discovered that the main design of the Germans was to strip away our divine image and to show the world that Jews were a subhuman species whose blood could be shed with no fear of punishment; that killing a Jew was like killing a fly: not only had no crime been commited, but you had done the world a favor by getting rid of a troublesome creature.

Part of their overall plan to develop a smooth-running machine for the annihilation of the Jews was the effort to instill in their victims a spirit of despondency so pervasive and deep that it would destroy whatever sense of hope we Jews might have, and leave nothing but broken shells to be led like cattle and sheep to the slaughter.

That is why I took it upon myself to encourage and inspire the brokenhearted, to inject within them the spark of hope, the belief that HaShem, the G-d of the Jews, would turn away His fury, heed our prayers, and not leave us in the hands of our enemies.

I organized a group of boys called Tiferes Bachurim, whom I taught Torah and the fear of G-d, implanting in them the seeds for eternal living that would sprout from doing G-d's will wholeheartedly.

Among the boys in the Tiferes Bachurim was an extraordinary boy from Kovno named Shereshevky who

---

1. *Tefilin,* phylacteries, are worn on one's head and arm in fulfilment of *Exodus* 13: 9 and 16, and *Deuteronomy* 6: 8 and 11: 18.

2. At the age of 13 a boy becomes obligated to fulfill all the Torah's commandments (mitzvos). The term means "bound by mitzva."

dedicated himself totally to the study of Torah. Even though he was not yet bar-mitzva, he was as precise as an adult in his fulfillment of *mitzvos*. This extraordinary boy asked me if he might be permitted to don *tefilin*, despite the fact that his bar-mitzva was 3 months away.

New edicts by the German taskmasters were issued against us every day; especially upon Jewish children. Who could assure this boy that he would ever reach the age of 13 to fulfill the mitzva? This was why he could not wait to don *tefilin*.

When I fathomed the simple sincerity of this boy's request, tears gushed from my eyes. I could not help citing the words of the prophet Yirmeyohu, "Who would grant that my head be water, my eyes a source of tears that I could day and night bewail the dead of my nation, for death has come up in our windows, has entered our houses, to destroy the youth outside, our chosen ones from the streets."

Response: I ruled that that precious child who had such a great desire to merit the privilege of fulfilling this mitzva because he feared that he might not live to fulfill it if he waited to reach 13, certainly had authorization for donning *tefilin*. I relied on the opinions that permit a minor to don *tefilin* if he knows how to guard them in cleanliness. This was certainly applicable to the Shereshevsky boy who had already demonstrated his fear of G-d and was a Talmud student aware and capable of maintaining the degree of bodily cleanliness required to don *tefilin*.

Moreover, since he was three months short of his thirteenth birthday, I relied on the prevailing custom that a boy dons *tefilin* 2 or 3 months before his bar mitzva.

Although I had ruled that he might don the *tefilin* even though he was still a minor, I warned him that if he should find himself with nine other Jews who wished to count him as the tenth for a *minyan*[3], he was obligated to let them know that he was not yet old enough to be counted into a *minyan*.

3. Quorum.

New edicts by the German taskmasters were issued against us every day; especially upon Jewish children. Who could assure this boy that he would ever reach the age of 13 to fulfill the mitzva? This was why he could not wait to don *tefilin*.

61: *The Right to Risk One's Life*

Question: The crowding in the Kovno Ghetto was unbearable. Within the tiny ghetto area some 30,000 people were incarcerated and every room had an inordinate number of tenants. No one was comfortable; every room had too many occupants. Understandably the filth was horrifying, and the hygienic conditions intolerable. The most important reason for the stench and the filth was the dearth of clothing; the ghetto prisoners, for the most part, owned no more than a single piece of clothing with which to cover themselves. People did not even own undergarments, and in the best of cases, a person had only a single shirt to his name, with no possibility of changing into something else. Nor was there any soap with which to bathe or launder their garments.

The third Egyptian plague ran rampant throughout the ghetto. Lice multiplied like ... lice! They crawled over people and into their garments. Nowhere in the ghetto were there any materials that could be used to clean people or their clothing or to destroy the despicable crawling creatures. The scratching caused people's skin to be filled with all kinds of sores, and people suffered intensely.

There was one area of respite for the ghetto dwellers and that was the bathhouse that the Germans allowed us to open there. The bathhouse had a special room where the heat was so intense that it killed all the crawling creatures in the bathers' garments. The bathers themselves would receive a small amount of liquid soap which was barely enough for them to wash their bodies, and left nothing over for laundering their garments. But then there was no place in the bathhouse for them to wash their garments; there was only the delousing chamber where the bathers placed their garments.

116

This bathhouse was especially important for ill and weak people. For the Germans did not recognize illness or weakness as sufficient excuse to free someone from slave labor. But when someone's turn came to go to the delousing center, and he received a note to that effect, then he was freed from work.

This was extremeley important for the ill and the weak.

I, the writer, was the bathhouse attendant, and I undertook this task joyfully. I did everything very precisely and made every effort to get enough wood to keep the delousing chamber functioning well. My goals were to provide the prisoners the opportunity to cleanse themselves from the great amount of filth and stench that clung to them because of the lack of hygiene in the ghetto situation, and to strengthen their weakened bodies by bathing. I thereby participated in making their suffering somewhat more bearable by lifting up their spirits.

More than once the great *gaon*[1] and *tzadik*[2], Rav Yehoshua Levinson — may G-d avenge him — director of the yeshiva in Radun and a grandson of the Chofetz Chayim — who remained alone in the Kovno Ghetto because his family was stuck in Radun — used to say to me, "I envy you because of this great mitzva that you are doing. Bathing in the bathhouse refreshes and instills in me the will to live, to merit seeing the consolation of the Jewish people and the downfall of the accursed Germans."

I utilized my position as bathhouse manager to keep the bathhouse closed on Shaboss and Yom Tov, even on winter Fridays and the days before Yom Tov. The head of Eltestenrat[3], Dr. Elchonon Elkes, warned me several times that my life was in danger if the Germans found out that I kept the bathhouse closed on Shaboss and Yom Tov without "justification." He also offered to provide me with another job. "Why do you insist on such a mean task, a bathhouse

1. Genius.
2. Righteous man.
3. Council of Elders.

attendant, which is not respectable for a rabbi? Besides, you are risking your life in keeping the bathhouse closed on Shaboss and Jewish holy days."

I explained to him that I was very pleased to be doing this because I saw it as a great privilege to cleanse Jews from the filth and to aid them hygienically. Another important aspect to this job was that it enabled me to aid escapees from the Ninth Fort.

In the Ninth Fort Jewish slave laborers were compelled to cremate — in mass graves — the bodies of the Jews who had been murdered by the Germans, as I describe in great detail in my work *Churban Lita (The Destruction of Lithuania)*. The slave laborers compelled to carry out this horrifying task knew very well that they too would be put to death by the Germans who systematically eliminated all traces and all witnesses of their genocide. Those unfortunate cremators took advantage of any opportunity to escape from the Ninth Fort to the ghetto. Unfortunately, they bore in their garments the stench of the dead because of their having to handle the corpses. As soon as they got into the ghetto their first stop was the bathhouse so that they could bathe their bodies and get the stench of the corpses out of their hair and skin. Their garments were not salvageable and had to be burned in the bathhouse boiler. After resting up for a while in the ghetto they would escape into the forest, in order to spread the word of what the accursed Germans were doing to the Jews in the Ninth Fort.

Once the German murderer Filgross — may his name be obliterated — came to inspect the bathhouse and found it closed on Shaboss. He asked, "Why is the bathhouse closed today? And where is the man in charge of it!"

Some ghetto prisoners heard about this and insisted that I open the bathhouse on Shaboss because of the danger to me in keeping it closed. But I paid no attention to them. When I later visted the Nachumovitch home to teach my regular students, they asked me if I had halachic sanction to endanger my life, for the Halacha is that only for three categories of transgression must one allow himself to be killed rather than transgress. How was I allowed to endanger myself in order to keep a different mitzva, in this case to observe Shaboss?

Response: I concluded that a person may risk his life for other *mitzvos*. The observance of Shaboss is a very great mitzva, equivalent to all the other *mitzvos*. Our sages said, "Whoever maintains Shaboss, it is ás if he has fulfilled the entire Torah. When one desecrates Shaboss it is as if he has denied the entire Torah." It was perfectly permissible for me to risk my life in order to keep Shaboss. I was within my rights in keeping the bathhouse closed, for to our great anguish and sorrow Shaboss was so desecrated in the ghetto that one could not know it was Shaboss. For the accursed Germans compelled the Jews to work even on Shaboss and Jewish holy days so that in the course of time Shaboss was almost entirely forgotten in the ghetto. I therefore found it proper to endanger myself to maintain Shaboss and sanctify it. I believe that thanks to this mitzva I survived the Vale of Tears and merited seeing the downfall of the evil Germans. "I thank G-d in my lifetime and praise Him while I live."

62: *Taking a Lulav[1] on the Sabbath*

Question: In 5703 (1943) when we were locked up in the Kovno Ghetto and Jews everywhere were being slaughtered, we hoped and prayed that ultimately the end would come to our troubles. As the month of Tishrey approached and the High Holy Days drew nearer, followed by the festival of rejoicing, Sukos[2], we grew more despondent and cried out to G-d, "How will we be able to fulfill the commandments of these holidays in the ghetto? Will the accursed Germans allow us to put up a *suka*[3]? Will a miracle take place and will we find an *esrog*[4] and a *lulav* to fulfill the mitzva of taking the four species as commanded by the Torah?"

When the holiday of Sukos arrived, our faces carried solemn, pained expressions instead of joy. Unable to fulfill the mitzva of the four species, we were especially disheartened because we did not know if we would ever again get the chance to fulfill this beautiful mitzva.

Suddenly a rumor spread through the entire ghetto that a Jew had just arrived from Vilna with a perfect set of the four species. Impossible! But true. This is how it happened: When the Germans took over factories in Vilna and in Kovno, they needed Jews who were experts on the machines and appointed them supervisors. From time to time, there were

---

1. A palm branch: see *Levicitus* 23: 40.
2. The festival of booths: see *Levicitus* 23: 23-44.
3. A temporary home built to fulfill *Levicitus* 23:42.
4. A citron: see *Levicitus* 23: 40. The other two species are myrtle and wilow twigs.

manufacturing breakdowns and the Germans would send these experts from Vilna to Kovno or from Kovno to Vilna, depending on the importance of the machine and the seriousness of the problem. These experts were guarded by Germans, whom it was sometimes possible to bribe to look aside and ignore what the Jewish experts might be carrying with them. More than once these specialists carried out vital missions in Kovno or Vilna.

One of these Jewish experts had just arrived from Vilna and had brought with him a rare *esrog* so that the Jews in the ghetto could fulfill the mitzva of the four species. Needless to say, our joy was great. But there was a catch; that year the first day of Sukos was a Sabbath — the one day on which it is forbidden to take the four species in hand. By German order, this Jewish expert had to return to Vilna immediately after the Sabbath. When the Jews realized that — despite the danger and sacrifice that went into getting the *esrog* and *lulav* into the ghetto — it would still be impossible for them to fulfill the mitzva, their anguish was great at having the mitzva stolen from underneath their noses. Their joy disappeared and left gloom in its wake.

And then the question was raised: might there not be some way to permit taking the *lulav* and *esrog* on the first day of Sukos even though it was Shaboss?

Response: After analyzing the situation and studying the reasons why the Sages forbade taking a *lulav* in hand on Shaboss in the first place, I considered that for the ghetto prisoners this Shaboss might unfortunately be the last opportunity to fulfill that mitzva, for who could know if he would remain alive to fulfill that mitzva again. It seemed to me that we could rely on the opinion of some of the earliest Sages who said that if one had taken a *lulav* on Shaboss he fulfilled the mitzva. In our circumstances, one could not say that a person who took the *lulav* was acting against the wishes of those Sages who originally forbade it.

Nevertheless, I was not inclined to rule that they should or should not take the *lulav* and *esrog* on that Shaboss. But because I did not specify the contrary, the Jews understood that the decision was up to them. As a result, many people rushed over to where the expert was staying and fulfilled the mitzva of *lulav* and recited the *shehecheyanu* blessing. Their eyes gushed with bittersweet tears at this opportunity to fulfill the mitzva, bitter because they were afraid that this might be the last time that they would hold a *lulav* in their hands, yet grateful for the gift of being able to fulfill the mitzva.

Happiest were the yeshiva students and other *bney*-Torah. A *chosid* of Lubavitch, Reb Feivel Zusman — may G-d avenge him — said to me, "I am fulfilling this mitzva without asking any questions. I am ready to suffer in *gehinom* for fulfilling this mitzva. All my life I spent large sums of money in order to purchase a perfect *esrog*, and now I am confident that this mitzva that I perform before my death will stand me in good merit when I come before the heavenly court."

Rabbi Avrohom DovBer Kahana-Shapiro, the rabbi of Kovno (who died in the ghetto on Shaboss 22 Adar I 5703 — February 27, 1943), was very ill at the time. Not only was he unable to fulfill the mitzva, but because of his illness it was impossible even to discuss the dilemma. When he improved, I visited him and told him what had happened, discussing various aspects of the problem. He asked me how I had ruled. I said that I had left the question open. He responded that even *lechatchila*[5] it had been permissible for the ghetto dwellers to recite the blessing on the *esrog* because the decree of the Sages forbidding taking the four species was inapplicable to the situation in the ghetto.

Some time later, while learning with my students at the Tiferes Bachurim group, I told them what the Kovno Rabbi had ruled, and they were extremely happy that they had truly fulfilled the mitzva of *lulav*.

---

5. Without reservation.

63: *Entrusting Jewish Children to Non-Jews*

Question: Before the Germans carried out their *Kinderakzion* to annihilate the Jewish children in the Kovno Ghetto on 3 and 4 Nissan 5704 — March 27 and 28, 1944 — word of the impending action got out. Mothers and fathers, knowing that the accursed murderers were planning to kill 1,200 Jewish children, sought every conceivable way to get their children away from the Germans or out of the ghetto.

One way was to acquire a birth certificate that showed the child had been born to non-Jewish parents, and then to place this certificate in the wrappings around the infant. The baby would then be left on the steps of a gentile orphanage or church to be raised as a foundling, the certificate proving the child was not Jewish.

Some Jews decided to hand their children over to gentile friends to be hidden until after the war with the stipulation that if the parents were still alive after the war the children would be returned to them. Others wanted to save their children so badly that they were even willing to hand them over to priests, although it meant that the children would not be raised as Jews. All they could hope for was that if their children survived, they might by G-d's grace find their way back to the Jewish faith.

I was asked if the Halacha permitted such actions since one could predict that few of the parents would remain alive, which meant that most of those children would be lost forever to the Jewish people.

Response: I ruled that parents might not give away their infant children to priests in order to save them from death at the hands of the German murderers. Although the children themselves had no obligation to fulfill the mitzva of sanctifying G-d, it is nevertheless forbidden for adults to hand them over to worshipers of idols.

As to the purchase of birth certificates made out to people with gentile names, see Response Number 58 on the subject of a passport with the initials R.C. in it.

As to people handing over their children to gentile friends or neighbors to be hidden until after the war to be returned to their real parents, there was legitimate concern that the children would be permanently lost for good among the gentiles. With life at stake, one must follow the lenient alternative. If the children were handed over to the Germans, they would surely be killed; but if they were handed over to the gentiles they stood a chance of remaining alive. It was also conceivable that the parents would survive. Even if the parents did not survive, it was possible that the gentiles would return the children to Jewish institutions after the war.

Since there were any number of possibilities, I ruled that we might be lenient and allow the anguished parents to hand over their children to gentile laymen in the hope that after the war they would indeed be returned to the Jewish people.

64: *Reciting Kaddish for Infants*

Question: After the Germans carried out the mass murder of Jewish children on 3 and 4 Nissan 5704 — March 27 and 28, 1944 — by butchering some 1,200 children and infants whom they tore from their mothers' bosoms and shot and burned, I was asked by the unfortunate parents whether they had the obligation to recite Kaddish[1] for their children and if there was any distinction to be made between infants and older children.

Response: I instructed the unfortunate parents to recite Kaddish for their beloved children, but only for those children who were 30 days old or more.

---

1. A prayer for the dead recited during public prayer sessions.

1944
to
Present

Horrors
unto the
Third
Generation

65: *Entering a Church*

Question: During the years in the Kovno Ghetto, parents who anticipated the annihilation of their children hastened to save their children by placing them outside the ghetto with non-Jews who agreed to take care of them until such time as their parents or other relatives claimed them.

Many Jewish children were placed with Catholic priests for safekeeping in churches and monasteries. The devout Catholics certainly hoped they would be able to win these souls for their faith. Therefore, immediately upon liberation, we hastened to make every effort to bring those children back from gentile hands and to restore them to the heritage of their parents.

Because many of those children were in the hands of priests, it became necessary to visit the priests in the churches in order to persuade them to return the children to Jewish hands. In many instances the presence of Jewish children was entirely denied with the claim, "We have no idea what happened to the Jewish children who were placed with us." Since there was a doubt as to whether the children were really there, might one enter the church to check on the presence of the children? By extension the question also applied to entering the rectories in which the priests lived next to the churches, because they kept relics and ikons there, and occasionally worshiped there too.

Response: Clearly, the intent of the Jews entering the churches was to save Jewish children from Christian worship. No one present would have thought that those Jews were, G-d forbid, entering the churches to worship there. I therefore ruled that they were to make every effort to enter the churches in order to seek the children and to restore them to their Jewish tradition and faith.

I did the same myself, personally visiting Lithuanian priests. Thank G-d, I succeeded in rescuing a number of Jewish children for Jewry. They are presently living in Eretz Yisroel, Torah-observant Jews in every respect.

66: *May Circumcision Follow Redemption of the Firstborn?*

Question: After the liberation we considered ourselves obligated to find every Jewish child who had been captured or hidden among non-Jews, particularly those whose parents had handed them over to gentiles in order to save them from German hands. I spared no effort in this sacred task of tracking down the children, even bribing the gentiles, for these children were the pure remnant, the sinless and blameless sheep, our sole consolation for the days of terror and fury we had so long endured.

Despite the danger that threatened those who wandered among the gentiles, many of whom hated Jews and were ready to shed their blood at a moment's notice, I could not restrain my sense of duty to seek out the little Jewish wanderers lost among them.

A number of the boys had not yet even been circumcised. Most were about 6 or 7 years old with no recollection of their parents, so it was impossible for them to tell us whether they were firstborn or not. Nevertheless, in many instances the parents had left letters in Yiddish and in Hebrew with the gentiles to whom they had entrusted their children, in which they provided specific details about their children, including names and family origins.

One boy's letter read that on the day the Germans entered Kovno, the boy's mother had given birth to him in the hospital. Immediately after the birth she gave her infant away to a gentile woman who had given birth at the same time. The gentile woman pretended that she had borne twins, and in this way saved the Jewish baby. In a letter that she had given to the gentile woman, the mother wrote

131

that the boy was a Jew and her firstborn son, so that whoever would read this letter in Yiddish would know that the boy had to be both circumcised and redeemed. I faced a procedural problem: Should the boy be circumcised first and then redeemed or should he first be redeemed and only then circumcised?

Response: After examining all the sources, I ruled that the boy should be circumcised before his redemption. I also ruled that the *sandak*, the man who holds the baby during circumcision, should be the one to recite the blessing, "Who has sanctified us through His commandments and commanded us to bring him into the covenant of our forefather Abraham."

67: *Mohel and Doctor in Conflict over Circumcision*

Question: After our liberation from the hands of the accursed Germans we began to seek out Jewish children, the future of the Jewish people, who had been placed in the hands of gentiles to be saved from extermination at the hands of the accursed Germans. I was among those who wandered throughout the villages and towns of the land seeking Jewish children in order to bring them back to the fold of Judaism.

Because of the danger, the ghetto dwellers did not usually circumcise their children inside the ghetto. Moreover, they hoped it would be easier to place uncircumcised children in the care of gentiles. At times, desperate parents even left their children in the doorways of gentile homes, in the hope that upon discovering that the children were uncircumcised they would assume the children were not Jewish.

Among the children I succeeded in rescuing was one three-year old boy who had not yet been circumcised. With great difficulty, we found a Jew who was a *mohel* (circumcisor). He came from the town of Staupitz in the Vilna district to circumcise 16 boys who had been saved from the gentiles.

When the *mohel* examined this child, he saw that he was very yellowish, and refused to circumcise him. A doctor was brought in to examine the boy and he determined that although the child was yellowish, he could still be circumcised. The *mohel*, however, stood firmly by his opinion and refused to circumcise the child. The problem I faced was this: We could not postpone this boy's circumcision for there were no other *mohalim* around, and this *mohel* was planning to leave the country shortly. Could

133

we, according to Halacha, rely on the doctor's opinion or not?

Response: After a very lengthy analysis of the halachic sources, I concluded that we could legitimately rely on the expert doctor we had brought in to examine the child. Nevertheless I decided to ask another pediatric specialist. I consulted a Doctor Rebelski who bore a particular love for Jewish children and had risked his life for them a number of times. Dr. Rebelski declared that there were four causes for the jaundiced look.

1: A certain dangerous blood type, which requires a total transfusion of all the blood in the body.

2: A sex-induced illness which is also dangerous to life.

3: An infection developed in the uterus; there is no treatment for this, children simply overcome the infection with the passage of time.

4: A reaction due to a secretion from the spleen; this also requires no treatment because the color passes with time.

As far as Doctor Rebelski could ascertain from his examination and the tests that he did on the child, this boy had none of those illnesses. Apparently, the gentile woman, who had fed him as well as she could, had not provided him with enough vitamins and other necessary nutrients and this deficiency had brought about the yellowness. Since all the tests had shown that the child was well, it was his opinion that the boy could be circumcised.

After hearing this second, expert opinion, I was inclined to rule that according to Halacha the boy could and should be circumcised. Such a ruling would be in accord with the opinion of Rambam (Maimonides). Yet, I preferred to avoid this ruling because the author of the *Shulchan Aruch* rules differently, and I feared risking even the slightest chance of danger to the child, for he was the only remaining survivor of his entire family which had been exterminated by the cruel Germans. If, G-d forbid, something should happen to the child as a result of this circumcision, we would be causing an entire family to disappear from the Jewish people. I therefore begged the *mohel* to postpone his departure from Lithuania, so as to be generous to the living as well as to the dead. The *mohel* agreed, putting off his trip until the child had completely recovered, the yellow color gone completely. Only then did the *mohel* circumcise the child, and the occasion proved to be the opportunity for a beautiful celebration.

One mitzva led to another. The story of the yellow boy and his circumcision had spread all over Kovno. A doctor in charge of a large hospital confided to me that he had a three-month old son whom he strongly desired to have circumcised.

At my request, the *mohel* also circumcised the doctor's son in secret, because Lithuania was then governed by the communists and if it was discovered that his son had been circumcised, this knowledge might have harmed the father. Our joy was truly doubled in the knowledge of having two circumcisions take place that same day.

68: *Anesthesia for Circumcision*

Question: After G-d liberated us from the cruel Germans who wanted to wipe out every last Jew, one of the first things we did was search the churches and monasteries for Jewish children who had been handed over to Christians to be saved. Those benefactors, not content with merely saving lives, had also "saved the souls" of the Jewish children by baptizing them and doing whatever else would help them forget their origins.

With great effort, dedication, labor, and suffering, we searched everywhere, in orphanages and even in private dwellings where we had information that a Jewish child might be living. Thanks to the One Above, we succeeded in this sacred work and gathered to us the remnants of our people who had been lost to us, bringing them back to their own people and to the faith of their forefathers.

Upon rescuing the children, we faced the problem of circumcising the boys whose parents had deliberately avoided circumcising them so that they could pass unnoticed among the gentiles. As a result of their deprivation and physical weakness, these children found it difficult to undergo the pain of circumcision. We spared no effort to help these youngsters understand the significance of the sacred commandment of circumcision, and proceeded to circumcise them according to Halacha. We were able to say to them, "Through your blood, in sanctity and purity, lives on the sacred people chosen by G-d as His treasure."

One boy of ten refused to be circumcised unless we could promise that he would not suffer pain. And so we considered whether an anesthetic might be used.

136

Response: I ruled that the circumstances in this case permitted the use of an anesthetic. Normally, to feel the same pain our forefather Abraham felt is considered a merit. But since Halacha does not mandate pain as part of the circumcision, there is no reason to impose it on the child.

Since the boy had already lived among the gentiles, if we violated his desire for painless circumcision, the possibility existed that he would rebel against the other commandments of the Torah and eventually choose to assimilate among the non-Jews. In that case, there could be no advantage in insisting that we perform the circumcision in the traditional manner, without an anesthetic.

My ruling was accepted. In a short period of time, we were able to circumcise some 80 children. Once they had entered the covenant of our forefather Abraham, each of them was a living memorial to his martyred parents killed in sanctification of G-d.

69: *Fulfilling One's Obligation to Recite Shema¹ by Hearing It*

Question: After the liberation, when I set out on my travels to seek out surviving Jewish children, I found a 14-year old lad in a village near the city of Pren wearing a cross around his neck. As soon as he saw me, he looked astonished, then removed the cross from his neck, threw it to the ground, and asked me, "Are there still any Jews alive in Kovno?

He said that he was a Jew and told me his given name as well as his family name. I asked him if he wished to come with me to live among his Jewish brethren. He responded that he wanted to, and immediately ran home to get his personal belongings. We set out together for Kovno, my heart pounding with joy at that rescue of a Jewish soul from among the gentiles.

Since his parents were not religious, the boy had received no Jewish education before the war. During the years he was hidden among the non-Jews his ignorance of Judaism, had grown no smaller. He had no concept of Jewish tradition. In Kovno, I placed him in the care of a family who taught him how to live as a Jew. They helped him get used to wearing *tzitzis²*, donning *tefilin³*, reciting *berachos⁴,* and in general inculcated in him a Jewish spirit.

1. *Deuteronomy* 6: 4-9 plus 11: 13-21, read twice daily in fulfilment of verses 6: 7 and 11: 19.

2. Tzitzis are the fringes attached to the four cornered garments worn by Jews in fulfilment of *Numbers* 15: 37-41.

3. *Tefilin,* phylacteries, are worn on one's head and arm in fulfilment of *Exodus* 13: 9 and 16, and *Deuteronomy* 6: 8 and 11: 18.

4. Blessing.

But with no knowledge of Hebrew and unable to read in a *siddur*[5], how could he in the meantime fulfill the important mitzva of reading Shema? Could he satisfy his obligation by hearing it read to him?

Response: I ruled that *Shema* should be read aloud in this boy's presence slowly enough for him to repeat every word. The *Shema* was not to be read to him while he merely listened passively, although Halacha allows this as a method of fulfilling the *mitzva*[6]. Our goal was to train him to fulfill the *mitzvos* himself. It was therefore better to have him repeat every word.

5. Prayerbook
6. Commandment (plural: *mitzvos).*

70: *Bar-Mitzva or Not?*

Question: After the Germans were defeated and the land was purged of its evil, the remaining Jews came out of the darkness of the ghetto and emerged alive from the hellish fires of the extermination camps. Many Jewish children were saved from the hands of the gentiles and brought back to their faith and raised again as loyal Jews with love for Torah and fear of G-d. I was asked the following question concerning one of those children who had remained alive thanks to the protection of the gentiles during the war years.

The boy's exact age was unknown, we could not determine whether he was 12 or 13 years old. All we knew was that his name was Yisroel Boruch and that his entire family had been destroyed by the Germans with the exception of an uncle who lived in South Africa and who could not tell us any more about the boy's age.

His teachers wished to know how to deal with his donning of *tefilin*[1]. Was he to be trained now because he might already be 13 years old and therefore obligated to don *tefilin* or were we to assume that he had not yet reached the age of *bar mitzva*[2] and was not obligated to wear *tefilin*?

Response: After studying the sources of Halacha on the subject, I responded that this young man should begin to don *tefilin* even though there was doubt whether he was 13 years old. Since he looked like he might very well be 13 years old, we had to concern ourselves with the possibility that he might already be obligated to don *tefilin*. Nevertheless I cautioned quietly that he not be included in a *minyon*[3] as one of the 10 men until we could say for certain that he was 13 years old.

---

1. *Tefilin,* phylacteries, are worn on one's head and arm in fulfilment of *Exodous* 13: 9 and 16, and *Deutronomy* 6: 8 and 11: 18.
2. *Age of obligation to perform mitzvos.*
3. Quorum.

71: *Self-Redemption[1] of a Firstborn Son*

Question: After the physical suffering of those in the Vale of Tears at the hand of the Germans came to an end, I took to the road to seek children living among the gentiles to bring them back to Judaism.

After many wearying searches, I tracked down a Jewish boy whose parents had left him with a non-Jewish family. In a letter left with the boy, his parents related that the child had been born in the ghetto, the scion of a respected family from the city of Tavrig in Lithuania. Circumcised according to Halacha, he had not been redeemed by a *kohein[2]* although he was his mother's firstborn child.

Years later, when he turned 13, knowing that he had not been redeemed, he wished to redeem himself. I pondered the question of whether it was appropriate for him to redeem himself now or whether he must wait because of the suspicion that he was still a minor who had not yet attained full physical puberty.

Response: I instructed the lad to wait until he attained full physical puberty at which time he would fulfill the mitzva.

---

1. The first born son of an Israelite must be redeemed by a *kohein*.
2. Every descendant of Aaron, the brother of Moses, is a *Kohein* (plural, *Kohanim*).

72: *A Father's Name for an Adopted Child*

Question: One of the most wicked acts of the Germans was taking the children away from their parents and butchering them, often in front of their very eyes. The mass murders of Jewish children were labeled *Kinderakzionen*, and their frequency brought deep anguish to Jews everywhere. In the Kovno Ghetto, the Germans organized the mass murder of Jewish children on 8 and 9 Teves 5704 — January 4 and 5, 1944. On those two days alone 1,200 children were slaughtered.

Miraculouly, one man managed to save a child from the murderers. He fed him and clothed him and raised him as if he were his own son. Through G-d's grace, both the man and the child survived the war.

Since he had no children of his own, the man wanted the boy to be considered his son in every way. When an *aliya* to the Torah is given, it is customary to call up the person by his own name and the name of his father. He came to me with the following question: When this boy would be called up to the Torah, could his, the adoptive father's, name be substituted for the natural father's name? An additional complication was that the child's real father was a *kohein*[1] while the adoptive father was not.

Response: I ruled that it was forbidden for the child to drop his real father's name. According to Halacha, the obligation to honor one's father continues from life through death, and one way men honor their parents after death is by being

---

1. Every descendant of Aaron, the brother of Moses, is a *Kohein* (plural, *Kohanim*).

142

called up to the Torah using the father's name. Calling this boy up to the Torah by the name of his adoptive father would preclude him from honoring his natural parents, and the failure to mention his father would constitute an insult to his memory.

Moreover, since the natural father was a *kohein*, if the boy were called up to the Torah in the name of the adoptive father, great confusion would ensue. With the passage of time it would be forgotten that the boy is a *kohein* and he might find himself violating transgressions proscribed for *kohanim* such as marrying a divorced woman or defiling himself with a corpse. In addition, he would not fulfill the *mitzvos* that are obligatory upon *kohanim* such as raising his hands to bless the congregants and being given the first *aliya* to the Torah.

I explained to the adoptive father that his reward would be very great without the recognition of having the boy called to the Torah by his name, for he had saved this child from death about which our Sages say, "Whoever maintains one Jewish life is considered as if he had maintained the whole world." G-d will doubtless reward him for his righteousness in raising the boy and educating him in the ways of goodness, and grant him great blessings and bounty.

73: *The Son Named After His Presumably Dead Father*

Question: On 28 Sivan 5701 — June 24, 1941 — the sun set at noon for the Jews of Lithuania. On that day the German army marched into Lithuania and the Jewish people, unable to escape their murderers, were put to the sword without mourning or burial. Wherever the Germans' butchering army arrived, pouncing suddenly, confusion and destruction came upon the Jews.

Many families were scattered and separated because the father or husband, son or daughter, had left on a trip just before the Germans arrived and all trace of them was lost.

Among the families so sundered was the Lieberman family. The father had left from Kovno to Vilna for several days. Meanwhile the Germans entered Vilna and, communications between the two cities cut off, his wife and infant daughter received no news of Lieberman. She had no idea whether he might still be alive or had been murdered by the accursed Germans.

A friend of theirs came to Kovno and told her that he had been in Vilna when the city was taken by the Germans and had escaped on foot together with hundreds of other Jews along the highway that led from Vilna to Kovno. Lieberman had been among the refugees. During their escape, however, German airplanes flew overhead and strafed the refugees with machine guns, and many of the refugees were killed. Since he did not see her husband again, the friend felt she could assume that he had been killed in the hail of bullets.

When the unfortunate woman heard this bad news, she mourned her husband and refused consolation for a long time. When the Germans conquered Kovno, she found a hideout for herself and her daughter among the gentiles and, in G-d's mercy, they both survived the war as did the son she bore, whom she named for her "late" husband.

Only when the Germans were finally defeated and the surviving Jews were able to come out of their hideouts, was Lieberman able to return from the Russian steppes where he had been exiled, and his wife's joy knew no bounds.

But when her husband discovered that his son had been named for him, he protested. He declared that under no circumstances would he consent to have his son bear the same name as himself. His wife's arguments that she had given the child the name in all innocence, thinking that her husband was dead, made no difference to him. He insisted that it is customary to give names to children in memory of the dead; since he was alive, he wanted his son to have a new legal name, so that the boy never would be called by his father's name.

I was then asked if it was proper to have the boy named for a living father, or whether his name should be changed in accord with the father's request.

Response: It was embarrassing to the father when others called his son by his name, for the father thought that he was being called. Moreover, when the father called his son using his own name, people who heard this thought it preposterous. Not realizing that he was calling his son, they thought he was talking to himself and that he was a lunatic. Furthermore, the father thought it was a bad omen for him if the son's name remained the same as his since it is our custom to give names in memory of the dead.

I therefore ruled that the father was right and the child should be given another name. Also that the name be legally changed in the birth register.

74: *Circumcising on Shaboss a Child Born to a Jewish Mother from a Gentile Father*

Question: After G-d took us, the prisoners of poverty, and removed from our backs the chains of slavery and then lifted us from the darkness and the shadow of death, I considered it as my foremost obligation to seek out the Jewish children still living among the non-Jews and to spare no effort in getting them out of non-Jewish hands into the fold of Judaism. I wandered through villages and hamlets seeking to redeem whatever Jewish children I could find, and to teach them the beginnings of G-d's wisdom, His Torah, and His commandments.

In the course of my wandering, I reached the town of Shadova, and was told that in a nearby village there was a Jewish girl living among the gentiles. I rushed to the village and found her there.

She was from a respected, well-to-do large scholarly family that had been completely destroyed. Only she from her entire large family had managed to stay alive, thanks to a gentile who had taken her into his home and raised her as if she were his own daughter.

But a thorn came with the rose: the gentile had a son who fell in love with the girl and wished to marry her. The father tried to persuade the girl to marry his son and undertook to provide for the couple's needs but she refused. One day, while she was alone, the son came into the house and raped her.

She now detested the gentile and his entire family, and wished to return to her own people. She knew that she had an uncle in the United States. Yet she had no idea how to go about getting out of Lithuania. At this point she didn't even know one Jew who might help her. In addition, she was pregnant, and felt embarrassed to be among Jews again.

Rabbi Ephraim Oshry

I consoled her and, once I understood the resilience of this young woman, I assured her that she would be accepted warmly and lovingly among Jews, and that many families would be pleased to adopt her as a daughter, and would consider it a great merit, a great *zechus*. G-d helped, and my words penetrated her heart and she agreed to come along with me. With great difficulty and at considerable expense I managed to get her away from the gentiles she was living with and bring her to Shavli where I arranged for her to live with a Jewish family of survivors. Some time later the family moved with her to Kovno, where she gave birth to a boy — on Shaboss.

The question then arose: Is it permissible to circumcise her son on the eighth day — Shaboss? Do we say that since the mother is Jewish, the child is considered Jewish and that his circumcision takes place on the Sabbath, or do we say that since the father is a non-Jew, he is not circumcised on Shaboss?

Response: I relied on the vast majority of the authorities who maintain that the fact that the child is "kosher" means that he is a Jew in every respect and may therefore be circumcised on Shaboss in accord with Jewish custom everywhere.

75: *Seeking Out the Murderers of One's Parents*

Question: After liberation, a man came to me with the following question: He knew that his parents, brothers, and sisters had all been killed by the Lithuanian janitor of the apartment house in which they had lived. He then discovered that the man was living in the city of Mariampol. Was he obligated to spend money and seek out the murderer in order to bring him to justice, so that other Jewhaters would learn a lesson and restrain their murderous instincts against the Jews?

That was a problem faced by many people. Many of the German murderers, along with their Lithuanian butcher-accomplices escaped to countries throughout the world and have never been brought to justice. To what degree were we obligated to make efforts to expose those murderers? Were we bound to avenge as much of the shed blood as possible? Or was one free to do what his heart and mind directed him to do?

Response: Although this matter had to be viewed in careful perspective to avoid creating fresh waves of anti-Semitism, one was certainly not to be apathetic, but to do everything he could to expose the murderers who had shed Jewish blood. We know today that many of them have changed their names and have gone underground so as not to be recognized.

I instructed the man to make every possible effort to avenge the murder of his family. Several weeks later he returned and told me that he had thrown a hand grenade into the janitor's house, killing him. I advised him to leave

Lithuania immediately so that the murderer's relatives should not find him, and also because the Lithuanian government did not look kindly upon Jews who took justice into their own hands. The man followed my advice and left the country.

76: *Reciting Mi Shebeirach[1] for a Gentile*

Question: When G-d had mercy on us and liberated us from our imprisonment, we who remained alive saw G-d's hand in our survival. One Jewish boy who had survived was brought by a gentile woman to the Kovno Jewish community. His parents had placed him in her care with a letter that included the address of their relatives in America. The woman requested that we do everything to place the child into the hands of his family. Great effort was made to trace the relatives, and the boy was received with open arms and all the love and sympathy that he needed to grow up as a true Jew.

Sometime later the gentile woman came to us with the following request: She had heard that the Jews have a custom of praying for sick people. And since she was very ill, she requested that we pray for her. She was confident that in the merit of her having rescued this boy, our prayers would be accepted and she would recover.

May Jews pray for or say a *Mi Shebeirach* for a non-Jew?

Response: I ruled that one might pray for this gentile woman. Prayer for her was certainly justified by her great act of generosity in saving a Jewish life. The ruling applied as well to reciting the *Mi Shebeirach* on her behalf.

---

1. A prayer for the recovery of a sick person.

77: *Burying the Bones of Martyrs*

Question: After the city of Kovno was liberated from the Germans and we came out of our hiding places, we discovered a horrifying scene — human skeletons, skulls, bones, and organs were lying about all of Kovno. From under the rubble of houses that the Germans had burned down in order to kill the Jews hiding in their basements and in the caves under the houses, charred human hands and legs protruded — evidence that there had indeed been hideouts in the buildings. The unfortunate Jews who had hidden there had been sentenced to death by simultaneous cremation and asphyxiation.

In the Ninth Fort, where some 40,000 Jews had been brought from all over Europe to be annihilated, we found on wooden pyres piles of gasoline-soaked corpses which the Germans had not had time to cremate. Wherever we dug, the shovels threw up bones and limbs of the dead. A number of problems arose concerning those remains:

1. Were we obligated to remove the bodies and the bones from wherever we found them to be buried in the Jewish cemetery of the ghetto or not? Halacha normally requires an unclaimed corpse to be buried where it is found. On the other hand, since these corpses were lying about like dung upon the earth, food for the birds and the wild animals, we feared that even those that were buried would be dug up by the scavengers. It thus seemed better to transfer them to a permanent burial-ground.

2. In exhumimg a body, Halacha requires that one dig three finger-breadths of soil around the body and bury that soil — which is assumed to contain decomposed flesh from

the body — together with the body in whichever burial-ground the body is reinterred. Was that *halacha* applicable to our situation?

Response: After considerable deliberation I ruled that corpses found under burned buildings should be taken together with the loose earth near them since, beyond a doubt, there was blood and flesh of the victims mixed in with that loose soil. Since the bodies had been lying around for a long time, some of the decomposed flesh had surely mingled with the earth around the bodies.

Since the extremely weak survivors did not have the strength to move the thousands of corpses and bury them properly in a Jewish cemetery, we survivors were able to get the government to put a number of German prisoners-of-war at our disposal to help us move the martyred corpses and bury them in the cemetery outside the ghetto.

And so we marched around from place to place, particularly in the Ninth Fort, collecting the bones and limbs of the martyrs which were lying all over. Because it was impossible to identify the bones and limbs as belonging to particular individuals, we buried them together in a collective grave, fulfilling in a sense the verse, "Those who were beloved and pleasant in life were not separated in death."

On the other hand, the clearly recognizable bodies pulled out from under the ruins of the houses were buried individually with a distance of at least one cubit between the graves. They were buried in their garments as found, and with the loose soil around them as required.

We fulfilled this great mitzva in the course of 6 weeks from 15 Menachem Av to 28 Elul 5704 — August 4 to September 16, 1944 — burying about 3,000 people. May the Redeemer of Jewish blood avenge them and wreak vengeance upon His enemies.

78: *Transferring Martyrs' Bones from a Non-Jewish Cemetery*

Question: When we undertook the awesome task of gathering together the remains of our holy martyrs killed by the murderous Germans during the holocaust years, we traveled from town to town where sacred Jewish communities had once flourished with Torah giants, scholars, rabbis, and great yeshivos. I saw how the land of Lithuania had betrayed its Jews; its people had collaborated with the German murderers and turned the country into a wasteland for Jewry.

I passed through the town of of Kupishok, hoping to find a trace of my mother and sisters. But woe unto me! All I found was destruction! The cemetery was unfenced, the graves of sacred ones unmarked and trampled by animals; and there were bones, dry unburied bones, strewn all over the cemetery. I was appalled that these Jews, desecrated once in their lifetimes, had now been desecrated again in death. I sought some way to bury the bones and kept thinking, "What if some of those unburied bones were the bones of my own mother, who raised me to study Torah and fear G-d and denied herself food to enable me to study Torah well nourished." Perhaps I would also find among the bones of the 3,000 holy Jews of Kupishok the Germans had murdered, the bones of my dear sisters and the bones of the rest of my family who were killed in sanctification of G-d!

I was shocked to discover that I was standing in the special cemetery for atheists that had been dedicated during the Russian conquest preceding the German occupation. Only a few people had been buried there before the Germans

153

began to use it for exterminating Jews. A question arose: Was it permissible to remove the bones from this place of murder to the Jewish cemetery for burial, because bones of non-Jews buried there earlier or non-Jews killed by the Germans afterwards might be intermingled with the bones of Jews?

Response: Since most of the people of Kupishok were Jews and almost all of them had been assembled on the atheists' cemetery to be be butchered by the Germans, we assumed that the vast majority, if not all, of the bones were Jewish. There was no question that the Germans had sought to annihilate only Jews, while the number of gentiles killed was extremely small. There was also no real reason to suspect that the Germans had dug up the graves of gentiles previously buried there. The bones on the ground could certainly be assumed to be those of Jews.

I therefore ruled that it was obligatory to collect all the sacred bones found on the surface of the atheists' cemetery and to bury them in a Jewish cemetery in accord with Jewish law. Besides fulfilling the commandment to bury a dead Jew to prevent disgrace and shame to the unburied body, this would terminate the insult to the Jewish martyrs whose remains had lain in the atheists' cemetery as if, G-d forbid, they had denied their Creator. We did everything in our power to remove these bones and bury them among Jews.

I further ruled that these sacred bones be buried in a special place, in accordance with the statement of *Maavar Yabok* (10): "Bury those who are murdered [by gentiles] separately because there is a constant Divine demand for justice which is not satisfied until the murderer's blood is shed, as is written, 'He who sheds the blood of a human being, his blood must be shed.' " I also required that a permanent memorial be placed upon the common grave of the bones so that future generations remember what the accursed evildoers destroyed and how much holy Jewish blood they shed. Earth! Do not cover their blood! It cries out to G-d from you and demands that G-d avenge it.

79: *Using Gold from the Teeth of the Dead*

Question: When G-d had mercy upon his suffering people and we were liberated, we discovered scenes that horrified even us. Skeletons and limbs, skulls and bones, were strewn like fertilizer on the ground of every corner of the concentration camp known as the Kovno Katzetlager. And from under the ruins of houses to which the Germans had set fire in order to root out the Jews who had been hiding in cellars and caves underneath, protruded the hands and feet and heads of scorched corpses.

Among the limbs and bones of our martyred brethren, we also found false teeth — some ceramic, some gold. I was asked if the Halacha permitted or forbade the use of such teeth and dentures.

There were two kinds: Bridges, which had filled the space between two teeth, and crowns, which were only gold plated. Having once been part of a dead body, might those crowns and bridges be used by the living? And what about bridges that had not been permanently attached, but were used only during the day for eating and cosmetic purposes. Were they considered part of the dead body or not?

Response: I forbade deriving any kind of benefit from those false teeth regardless of whether they were removed as often as twice a week to be cleaned or whether they were never removed at all. I forbade as well any use at all even of dentures that had been used solely for cosmetic purposes and were removed every single night.

80: *Reinterring a Jewess Buried Among Gentiles*

Question: After the liberation, a Mrs. Goldberg of Vilkovisk came to me with a question that troubled her greatly. During the Holocaust years her daughter had managed to hide among gentiles. Disguising herself as a gentile, she had attended their church and worn a cross, had eaten and drunk with them, and had acted like a gentile woman in every respect. When she had taken ill and died, she was buried in the gentile cemetery. Mrs. Goldberg strongly desired to exhume her body and reinter it in a Jewish cemetery.

Response: Since the woman's entire purpose in acting as a non-Jewess was simply to save her life, there is no doubt that whatever she did was done secretively so that no non-Jew would discover that she was Jewish. Nor did she reveal her secret to Jews. Even if one or two members of her family might have been aware of her secret, certainly neither she nor those relatives would have told anyone else lest it eventually reach the ears of the gentiles who would not have hesitated to hand her over to the Germans to be killed.

I therefore assumed that no ten Jews had known that she was acting as a gentile. Consequently, she was not considered a public transgressor, rather one who transgressed out of compulsion. This put us under obligation to concern ourselves for her honor and not to allow her to remain dishonored in death by being buried among non-Jews. It was mandatory that she be exhumed and reinterred in a Jewish cemetery where her remains would repose with all the other martyrs who died sanctifying G-d, to arise with them all at the Resurrection.

156

81: *Using a Gravestone with a Cross*

Question: During the days of horror, when the Jewish people were held in the grip of the German butchers, everyone sought a way to escape certain death. Many Jews disguised themselves as non-Jews. Among them was a Jew who did everything to make it seem that he was a gentile. He attended church, wore a cross, and behaved just as the gentiles did so that no one should suspect him of being Jewish.

When the man died, he was buried in a Christian cemetery. After the liberation, his brother arrived and removed the body from the Christian burial ground, and had his brother reinterred in a Jewish cemetery.

One last thing he wanted to do for his late brother was to place a tombstone on his grave. Since he could not afford to purchase a stone and since he was planning to leave the blood-soaked soil of Lithuania never to return, it occurred to him to take the tombstone that had rested on his brother's grave in the Christian cemetery, erase the cross that was etched on it, and replace it with his brother's name. I was asked if that was permissible.

Response: Since the tombstone originally came from this man's grave, there is no reason to forbid placing it upon his new grave in the Jewish cemetery. The cross had been carved by non-Jews for a man they thought was a gentile. Had they known he was Jewish, they would never have put a cross on his tombstone. There was thus no reason at all to forbid the re-use of that stone.

82: A Tombstone that Does not Mark a Grave

Question: After G-d spared the remnants of the ghetto, I wandered through the ruined cities of Lithuania to seek out my remaining brothers and sisters, one from a city and two from a family. In town after town, community after community, I found that the Jews had been wiped out completely. The entire countryside was marked with mass graves. Not only had the enemy been merciless in annihilating men and women, young and old, but he had also destroyed the cemeteries where the dead of previous generations had lain in peace. In almost every town of Lithuania, tombstones had been overturned and, in many cases, the cemeteries plowed under.

A Mr. Segal, one of the survivors, came to me with the following question. His parents had been fortunate enough to die before the Holocaust and had been buried in the communal cemetery in Ponievezh. But the defiling evildoers had desecrated everything holy there, had upset the tombstones and destroyed the graves. Furthermore, the ledger of the burial society had disappeared, so that he had no way of locating his parents' graves. He wished to know if he might set up a stone in memory of his parents somewhere in the cemetery.

Response: I ruled that it was permissible for him to put up a tombstone for his parents anywhere in the cemetery, and that he should inscribe words on it to the following effect, "My father _____ and mother _____ are buried in this cemetery, but during the Holocaust the wicked evildoers caused their graves to be lost." In this manner the stone

158

would serve both the dead and the living, because the main reason for placing a tombstone on a grave is so that the person buried there should not be forgotten by the living. It is therefore irrelevant whether one places the tombstone exactly on the grave or at some distance from it.

This particular stone, not over a grave, would cause the dead to be remembered even more when passersby see that it is different from all the other tombstones. For people pay more attention to and talk more about the unusual than the usual. By setting up such a stone in the cemetery he would keep his parents' names from being forgotten by the living.

For the living too such a stone would be of value, because visitors would be able to pray next to it even though it is not precisely on a grave. One may pray at any point in the cemetery.

83: *Using Trees from a Cemetery*

Question: After the liberation I wandered through the ruined towns of Lithuania — where communities of Jews had lived and had offered up their lives to sanctify G-d — in order to seek out the burial places of our martyred brothers and sisters who had been mercilessly murdered by the accursed malefactors. Everywhere I visited, the Lithuanians showed me the mass graves into which the murderers had cast the sacred bodies of our brothers and sisters after murdering them in the most horrible fashion. There were places where the people had been cast into pits alive, and were then covered over with soil while they were still breathing.

I perceived that most of the mass graves were in pastures and fields. I feared that the owners of the fields might plow over the graves when sowing their fields, and that with the passage of time the graves would be totally obliterated. To keep the farmers from pasturing their animals there and from plowing over the graves, I wished to put fences around these mass graves so as to preserve them and to ensure that our martyrs would rest in peace.

But there was no way I could afford to purchase the boards to make the fences. And so I pondered whether it might be permissible to use trees growing in the Jewish cemeteries and to make fences out of that wood to protect the graves of our martyrs.

Response: After considerable study I concluded that the trees standing nearest the fences of the cemeteries could be used, because those trees were most likely not rooted in graves. I also instructed that these trees not be cut down to

160

their roots but to their trunks. This ruling was followed in many towns in Lithuania, where the trees from the cemeteries were used to make fences around the mass graves of our martyred brethren.

But all our work was in vain, because the cruel Lithuanians who had assisted the German butchers in murdering our brothers and sisters broke down the fences we had put up with so much labor and effort, so that all signs of their participation in the murder of our people might be eradicated in order that they might be able to say, "We have done no evil."

The same fate that awaited the mass graves of the Jews throughout Lithuania also awaited the field where the Jews were murdered in the Ninth Fort next to Slobodka. There the remains of some 40,000 Lithuanian, German, Austrian, and French Jews had been buried. This grave was plowed under and planted in potatoes and grain. This produce, fertilized by the blood of our martyred brothers and sisters, was eaten by the Lithuanian peasants, the cruel murderers who had helped the accursed Germans annihilate these Jews and who had robbed them.

Recall, O G-d, what happened to us and avenge the blood of our martyrs before our very eyes!

84: *A Sidewalk Paved With Jewish Gravestones*

Question: The land of Lithuania was covered in darkness and its Jewish inhabitants, who had built up the country with their sweat and genius during the hundreds of years they had lived there, were destroyed by the cruelest enemy in modern history. When we were finally liberated from this darkness, we were shocked to discover that the poisonous tentacles of this destruction had reached even the cemeteries where our ancestors lay buried. Imagine the torment we felt when we discovered that the streets under our feet were paved with gravestones bearing the names of the Jewish dead accompanied by descriptions testifying to their righteousness and saintliness.

I was asked how a Jew should treat these stones and if he was permitted to step on them or not.

Response: So long as the inscriptions on those stones were visible and legible, there was no greater desecration to the memory of the dead than allowing them to be stepped on by people or trampled by animals with mud and manure clinging to their hooves. For a Jew, a descendant of Jacob, to walk on those stones and thereby add further shame and embarrassment to his own dead was clearly forbidden. The shame was great enough without that.

We were assured by the municipality that every effort would be made to have the gravestones pulled up from the street and placed in a protected area, but not in a cemetery, because most cemeteries were not recognizable. They had been plowed and turned into gentile pastureland. These gravestones were to be placed only in existing cemeteries which were still protected by fences.

Since our city of Kovno still possessed an undestroyed cemetery, we spared neither money nor effort to transfer all the tombstones from the rest of Lithuania to this last surviving cemetery and arranged a special area inside it. These dug-up tombstones became a monument for future generations to the pathology of German hatred. May their memory be eternally damned but their evil remembered forever, an evil that not only destroyed millions of Jews but disturbed the rest of hundreds of thousands of the dead. Remember O, G-d, what has been done to us, and avenge the blood of Your servants!

85: *Reciting Kaddish[1] for a Gentile Woman*

Question: During the days of affliction when the accursed Germans mercilessly annihilated young and old, men and women, the Lithuanian gentiles, with whom the Jews had lived for hundreds of years, conspired with the German murderers to kill Jews and loot their property. They sought out the Jews wherever they were hiding and whenever they caught one immediately handed him over to their German masters who proceeded to torture and kill the Jew.

Despite the violent hatred that the gentiles had for the Jews, a hatred which the Germans fanned into a flame of vengeance, there were among them unique individuals who were anguished by the cruelty committed against Jews and would not sit by doing nothing. Whatever they did, though, was done at an enormous risk because the Germans immediately shot anyone they suspected of aiding Jews. Nevertheless, such people existed and they saved Jews at whatever cost.

In 1945, shortly after our liberation, Reb Moshe Segal came to me with the following question: He had been saved by a gentile woman who, at enormous risk to herself, had hidden him in her basement together with ten other Jews, providing them all with food and shelter until the liberation. After the war, when these Jews wanted to repay her in some way for her great compassion, they discovered to their deep sorrow that she had died right after the liberation. The idea took root in their minds to say Kaddish for her, and Reb Moshe Segal was chosen for the task. His question was whether it is permissible to say Kaddish for a gentile?

1. A prayer for the dead recited during public prayer sessions.

Response: Basically, Kaddish is a prayer of praise to G-d. When Rabbi Nathan of Babylonia was appointed Exilarch, the cantor used to add in Kaddish the phrase, "In your lifetime and in your days and in the lifetime of our Exilarch and in the lifetime of all the Jewish people." Similarly, in the days of Maimonides, they used to add in the Kaddish, "In your lifetime and in the lifetime of our master Moshe ben Maimon." In this vein of mentioning others in the Kaddish, it is plainly permissible to say Kaddish in memory of the gentile woman who saved so many Jews from death. The work *Sefer Chasidim* teaches that it is permissible to ask of G-d to accept favorably the request of a non-Jew who has done favors for Jews. And saving his life is the greatest favor that one can do for a Jew. Not only is it permissible to say Kaddish with her in mind, it is a mitzva to do so. May He Who grants bounty to the Jewish people grant bounty to all the generous non-Jews who endangered themselves to save Jews.

86: *Burying the Remains of Torah Arks*

Question: My soul weeps when I recall the desecration of Kovno's hundreds of synagogues and houses of study, particularly the world-famous Yeshiva Knesses Yisroel in Slobokda-Kovno, one of Jewry's most important centers where Torah and *mussar* were studied and taught for over 50 years. Woe unto us for whom the sound of Torah has ceased in Slobodka! the sound of Torah that echoed from one end of the world to the other!

The Germans and their assistants, the accursed Lithuanians, razed this Torah center to its foundations. They entered the Yeshiva Knesses Yisroel, this sacred domain of G-d, and defiled its character, not because of their own power but because G-d's fury was released against His people and He placed Jacob and Israel in the hands of the German beasts — may their name be obliterated — thus fulfilling the verse, "Let us go annihilate them from being a nation; let the name Israel no longer be mentioned."

After G-d remembered the scattered remnants of His people and brought about the downfall of the German evildoers, we saw, to our great shock, the ruined building of the yeshiva. Even the location of the sacred ark in which the Torah scrolls had always been kept was no longer recognizable.

It seemed that the Germans had vented their wrath on this particular place more than on any of the other sacred places in the town. The yeshiva, a symbol of the guidance of Torah in Lithuania for over 700 years, was a sore to their defiled eyes. They destroyed it totally.

We searched among the ruins for other yeshivos and synagogues which could still be used for prayer or study, and were shocked by the utter destruction. Most of the holy places were empty ruins, nothing but roofless walls and broken windows, and the rest had been turned into stables by the accursed Germans and their Lithuanian helpers. Only here and there did a piece of synagogue furniture turn up. In some we found that the ark or part of it had remained intact; but in most of them all we found was a wall bookcase or some other piece of built-in furniture. The question then arose whether those remnants of sanctity required burial or not.

Response: In those synagogues or yeshivos in which nothing remained, not even a fragment of the holy ark, except for the space the ark had occupied, there was no question that the place had no particular sanctity. But where part of an ark survived, then the remaining boards had to be hidden or buried to preclude their use for any less sanctified purpose. But any other surviving furniture, such as bookcases, required no special treatment.

87: *An Ark Curtain Used by a Non-Jew*

Question: When G-d, in His great mercy, defeated the German enemy and we crawled out of our hiding places through the reopened gates of the ghetto, our joy was wiped away by the scenes of destruction that greeted our eyes. Synagogues and houses of study had been burnt, holy places destroyed. There was simply nowhere we could pray in public. Kovno, which had once been a great Jewish city, was bereft of her children, of her scholars.

The one place that looked as if it could be turned back into a house of prayer was the Hoisman Kloiz. But it was filled with filth left deliberately by the accursed Germans. With great effort we scraped clean this holy place in order to restore a measure of its original glory and sanctity. When we finished, we discovered to our sorrow that we did not have a curtain for the ark. And, because the Germans had looted every single inch of cloth in Kovno, there was nothing to use for sewing a new curtain for the ark.

One Jew recalled that he had seen the ark curtain from the Merchants' Synagogue being used in a gentile house as a bedspread. I was asked whether this use constituted a desecration of the ark curtain, and if it did, whether that desecration made it unfit for further use as an ark curtain should we succeed in reclaiming it.

Response: The gentile's use did not constitute a desecration of its original sanctity, and it was therefore definitely permissible to use the curtain as the cover of our ark.

88: *Utilizing the Cover of a Torah-Scroll*

Question: A respected member of the community came to me after liberation and presented the following problem:

His family had held onto a precious heirloom for 300 years, a Torah-scroll written in a beautiful script. It was unusually tall, much taller than most Torah-scrolls found in synagogues, and its cover was an exquisite example of Jewish craftsmanship. To the family it was worth more than a fortune in gold.

During the days when the accursed murderers furiously destroyed all the Torah-scrolls and sacred books they could get their hands on, they tortured this man's father and forced him to burn his family heirloom, the old and unusually tall Torah-scroll. But before the Germans could get their hands on the exquisitely crafted cover, the son managed to hide it.

Now that the son had, through G-d's mercy, miraculously survived, he wished to donate his rare Torah-scroll cover to a synagogue. At the same time, his own son was about to become a *bar mitzva*[1] and would soon fulfill the beautiful mitzva of donning *tefilin*[2]. Since the man wanted to retain within his family some memento of their splendid Torah-scroll, he was considering the possibility of shortening the Torah cover to fit a normal-sized Torah-scroll, and using the

---

1. At the age of 13 a boy becomes obligated to fulfill all the Torah's commandments (*mitzvos*). The term means "bound by mitzvos."
2. *Tefilin*, phylacteries, are worn on one's head and arm in fulfilment of *Exodus* 13: 9 and 16, and *Deuteronomy* 6: 8 and 11: 18.

remnant of the cloth to sew a *tefilin* bag for his son's *tefilin*. His question was whether turning a Torah cover into a *tefilin* bag is considered a desecration?

Response: I ruled that the extra cloth should simply be hemmed up inside the cover of the Torah-scroll. To do otherwise would mean cutting away a part of its sanctity. The scroll cover was to be used in its entirety; I forbade cutting off any extra cloth, even for so ostensibly noble a purpose as turning it into a *tefilin* bag.

89: *What to Do With Fragments of a Torah-Scroll*

Question: After our release from bondage after the German defeat, we were shocked to discover the desecration the accursed Germans and their assistants had wrought upon our Torah scrolls which they had robbed from our synagogues. They had turned the holy parchment into shoes; and in the villages of Lithuania the farmers had plastered their kitchen and bedroom walls using the parchment as wallpaper; and the sacred words of Torah, including G-d's sanctified name, could be found all over the streets and in the garbage pits of Lithuania.

A man came to me with the following question. Descended from the *Gaon* of Vilna, his family had owned and carefully guarded a Torah-scroll that had once belonged to the *Gaon* himself. Before the questioner was locked up in the Kovno Ghetto he had hidden this scroll in a secret place. After the liberation, he returned and discovered that the hiding place had been found: the Torah-scroll had been cut to pieces by malicious desecrators. He wanted to know if he might be allowed to keep the remaining fragments of the Torah-scroll inside his house in order to preserve the heritage of his family which had constantly cared for this Torah-scroll, and also to have it serve as a memorial to those members of his family who had been killed by the accursed Germans. Or was he obligated to remove the cut-up fragments of the Torah-scroll to a *geniza*, the customary hideaway?

Response: The questioner is allowed to keep the fragments of the Torah-scroll in his house, since the entire purpose of *geniza* is to protect the honor of the Torah-scroll which

171

would be considered desecrated or shamed if it were not kept in a protected place. Since the questioner seeks to preserve the Torah-scroll and to guard the fragments as a memorial to the members of his family who were exterminated by the accursed Germans, this is certainly the most fitting type of *geniza* for these fragments. I instructed the man to see to it that the place he set aside for those fragments in his home be in a room not used for sleeping.

90: *The Sunken Torah Scroll*

Question: Immediately after the liberation, when G-d opened the gates and redeemed us from our bondage, a respected Lithuanian Jew poured out his heart to me. He related how he had seen the Germans bait an old rabbi and, under pain of death, force him to burn a Torah-scroll with his own hands. Since the witness owned a Torah-scroll himself, he began to worry lest they compel him to burn his Torah-scroll too. He woke up in the middle of the night, took his Torah-scroll to the river and let it sink to the bottom to keep the accursed Germans from desecrating the sanctity of the Torah.

Nevertheless, he was troubled by doubts: Why hadn't he found another way to hide the Torah-scroll? And who could say for certain that the Germans would have compelled him to burn the Torah-scroll? And even if they would have compelled him to do exactly what they had forced the old rabbi to do, by what right had he assumed that he was allowed to throw the Torah-scroll into the depths of the river before the problem actually came up? And which was more disgraceful — throwing the Torah-scroll into the river or burning it?

After liberation, the first thing he did was hurry down to the river in the hope of dredging up the Torah-scroll from the bottom so that he could bury it in the traditional manner. But his efforts were in vain; he could not locate it. Then he came to ask whether he needed to atone for his action.

Response: When this man had cast the Torah-scroll into the river, he had done so out of respect for its holiness and a

173

clear desire to save it from further abuse. He was therefore not obligated to atone for his deed. But I suggested that when G-d, in His bounty, granted him prosperity, it would be appropriate for him to set aside money and purchase a Torah-scroll through which he would sanctify G-d and remedy an act of desecration brought about by the accursed Germans.

91: *Erasing Transferred Torah Script*

Question: The Germans looted the Jews' property and harmed us physically. Even more significantly, they sought to destroy the spirit and the heart of the Jewish people. This is why they vented their fury on Jewry's great leaders and scholars and on the beloved, holy Torah scrolls for which we sacrificed out lives. After the liberation, there was not a single Torah scroll to be found in Kovno except for a small Torah which I kept with me wherever I went, guarding it as if it were my own eye. They burned some 500 Torah scrolls, scrolls originally from Kovno and Slobodka and many surrounding towns and cities such as Aleksot, Shantz, and Panamen.

Woe unto the eyes that saw a major Jewish city like Kovno, once filled with sages and scholars, synagogues and study halls, now bereft of Torah!

In addition, we saw with our own eyes how the non-Jews defiled the Torah scrolls. Many of them ripped the sacred sheets of parchment and turned them into shoes. Torah! Torah! Don sackcloth and mourn your beauty which has been trampled into the earth! And your sanctity which has been desecrated by the accursed Germans and their assistants, the Lithuanians!

Shortly after the liberation, a sexton named Reb Reuven found a Torah scroll wrapped in silk and other pieces of cloth hidden in a cellar. As a result of the dampness, a number of letters from the Torah had been impressed on the silk and then from the silk back onto the scroll. In addition, a number of letters from the Torah scroll itself had been transferred to the back of the parchment. Was it permissible to erase these letters?

Response: There is no ban against erasing a non-letter. Since the letters transferred from the scroll onto the back of the parchment were reversed, I ruled that they might certainly be removed. However, those letters that were impressed from the scroll to the silk and from the silk back onto the scroll, and were thus perfectly readable, might not be erased.

92: *Torah Scrolls, Tefilin, and Mezuzos Found in the Possession of Non-Jews*

Question: After G-d liberated us from the ghetto, we began to seek out the survivors and the children. We also sought out any surviving sacred works, such as Torah scrolls, *tefilin¹* and *mezuzos²*, all of which were rare and in great demand. While searching we discovered that many gentiles posessed *tefilin* from the days when they had looted Jewish homes and murdered the inhabitants. I was asked whether one might immediately don *tefilin* taken back from the gentiles without waiting for an inspection to check whether they were kosher or not?

Response: If they are old *tefilin* it is permissible to don them, because one can see they were once used, and there is no need to wait until an expert examines them. Our situation was such that there were so few pairs of *tefilin* available that if the *tefilin* had to be examined first, and their owner compelled to wait, he would have to be without *tefilin* for a while. No substitute pairs were available. When I ruled that they might don these *tefilin*, the just-liberated Jews cried with joy.

1. *Tefillin*, phylacteries, are worn on one's head and arm in fulfilment of *Exodus* 13: 9 and 16, and *Deuteronomy* 6: 8 and 11: 18.

2. *Mezuzos* (singular, *Mezuza)* are parchment scrolls containing two paragraphs from *Deuteronomy*, 6: 4-9 and 11: 13-21. which are attached to the doorposts of a Jew's home.

93: *Torah Volumes Abused by Gentiles*

Question: After G-d rescued the remnant of the Jews from the hands of the cruel Germans, we were shocked to see the devastation that had been wrought throughout Lithuania by the Germans and their Lithuanian helpers. A country that had been famous for its Torah institutions was now a wasteland. We, the surviving brands plucked from the fire, sought to re-establish our lives as quickly as possible, and discovered that not only had the German butchers systematically annihilated the Jewish people, but they had furiously and consistently destroyed all our sacred works. For it was impossible to find a single *chumash[1], gemara[2]* or *siddur[3]* in the entire city of Kovno after the liberation.

Some weeks after our liberation, I came across a number of crates filled with Jewish works in a storeroom. These books had once belonged to the Jews of Hamburg, and the accursed Germans had expelled the Jews of Hamburg from the city in which they had dwelt for generations by telling them that they were resettling them in the East, in Lithuania, and that they were therefore to take with them all their possessions. These unfortunate Jews, misled by their murderers, packed all their possessions, including the sacred *seforim[4]* they owned. Eventually they discovered that the cruel Germans

1. Pentateuch
2. Talmud volume
3. Prayerbook
4. Books

178

had lied to them. They were all brought to the Ninth Fort outside Kovno where the cruel murderers shed their blood. The Jews of Hamburg were put to death here along with their brethren from other cities and other countries. All the possessions they had taken with them were looted by the murderers including the sacred books in the storeroom in the fortress.

Understandably, when I discovered the *seforim* of the Hamburg Jews I rejoiced and had them taken into the Hoisman Family Kloiz (a small synagogue) so that they would be available to others who wished to study Torah. When I brought these books into the *kloiz*, the sexton, Reb Reuven, burst into tears and told me how he had seen non-Jews in the marketplace wrapping fish and other objects in pages taken from *gemaros* and other sacred texts that had been brought to Kovno from the warehouses of the Romm printing house in Vilna. The questions that arose were whether we were obligated to redeem the pages from the hands of the non-Jews so that they should not be treated disrespectfully and — if we redeemed them — what were we to do with those pages, for they were certainly in no condition to be used for studying.

Response: I ruled that we were definitely obligated to redeem them from the non-Jews so as to prevent even inadvertent erasure of the Divine Name. Our sacred Jewish brethren, upon learning of this obligation to redeem the pages from the non-Jews, saved up their pennies and redeemed all the pages from the non-Jews. I then followed the custom prevalent in Lithuania, instituted by the sage Rav Yitzchok Elchonon Spector of Kovno, to have all the old and torn pages placed in sacks, brought to the cemetery, and buried in a special **wood-lined grave.**

94: *Returning Sacred Works to Their Owners*

Question: On the first of Adar 5702 — February 18, 1942 — the Germans ordered the Jews dwelling in the darkness of the ghetto to give up every single book they possesed, both sacred and secular. The Jewish police inside the ghetto, under a special order, were responsible for the gathering of these books inside a special depot established by the Germans. Whoever disobeyed would be put to death. Understandably, Jews began to bring their books to the designated warehouse.

From all over the ghetto, from synagogues as well as from private libraries, the books arrived. Among the collections was the vast library of Rabbi Yitzchok Elchonon Spector, one of the great teachers of all Jewry, who had been Rav of Kovno till the 1890's.

An official in the Jewish ghetto police, Mr. Yitzchok Greenberg — may G-d avenge him — took advantage of this opportunity and, at great risk to himself, selected the most precious volumes of the great rabbi's collection and hid them inside a box which he buried in a deep pit, hoping that when G-d's mercy returned to His people and He raised them from under the German yoke, this hidden treasure would be discovered and the sacred works inside brought to light.

And so it was. When the Jews of the ghetto were liberated, they began to dig within the ghetto walls for the wealth they had hidden from German eyes. One of the diggers found this box of precious books and, under the impression that the books were his personal property because he had discovered them, rejoiced at his great find.

When the news spread, many survivors came to feast their eyes upon the holy books. One man recognized books from his own collection among the find, books that bore his own signature and the signatures of his grandfather and father, precious heirlooms that had been passed down from generation to generation. He demanded the return of his family's property. But the finder claimed that this was legitimately found property whose original owners had given up hope of ever retrieving it; that the situtation was no different than if he had found the books at the bottom of the ocean. I was asked by both parties to settle the matter in accordance with Torah law.

Response: I ruled that according to Halacha those books belonged to the man who had found them. First of all, the original owners had given up hope of ever retrieving the books. There was no question that the ghetto dwellers knew that whatever the Germans put their hands on was forfeit. Even their very lives were held in the grip of the German fist to play with as long as the Germans pleased. Secondly, when those books were later found they immediately passed into the possession of another party — the finder. It was therefore clear to me that those books belonged to the man who had dug them out of the ground.

95: *Using a Paroches for a Chupa*

Question: On 13 Menachem Av 5704 — August 2,1944 — ,
the surviving Jews were liberated. Although the threat of
death had been removed, we were shocked to see that every
sacred object had been trampled underfoot; most of the
synagogues and houses of study in Kovno had been razed,
and the few that remained had been turned into stables.
There were no Torah scrolls or any other sacred works
available for public use, with the exception of my personal
small Torah scroll which I had preserved by keeping it with
me wherever I went.

A few weeks after the liberation, we celebrated the
wedding of a man and woman who had survived the war.
Because we could find no other cloth to use as a *chupa*
(wedding canopy), I was asked whether we might use a
paroches (curtain for a Torah-ark) which we found in the
attic of the Hoisman Kloiz.

Response: I allowed using the *paroches* for a *chupa*,
because we had no other cloth to use.

96: *The Child of a Jewish Woman and a Non-Jew*

Question: After G-d liberated us from the German enemy, we made every effort to support each other so that we would not break down at the sight of the total destruction of Lithuanian Jewry whose rootedness in Lithuania for hundreds of years did not keep it from being smashed to pieces when the hurricane came.

We never imagined that the Lithuanians, who had benefited so much and so long from Jewish talent and labor, would turn against us and help the German murderers perform their cruel selections. We had hoped that even if the Lithuanians would not help us openly, they would at least do so secretly. Our disappoinment was great. The Lithuanian farmers turned their backs on an entire people who had been good to them over the generations and who had rebuilt their nation after World War I — and proceeded to help the destroyers loot defenseless Jews. Like loyal dogs, they licked the boots of their German masters and betrayed individual Jews who had managed to hide underground, in forests, and in the homes of friendly gentiles. As soon as they had the slightest suspicion that someone was a Jew, they immediately surrounded him like hounds and handed him over to their German masters.

Moreover, the priests and the nuns of the "religion of love" rubbed their hands with delight when they saw the Jews suffering — as they professed — for crucifying the Jew they worshiped. The only Jews they had mercy on were Jewish children whose souls were there for saving. Believing these children to be the property of their faith, they regarded it as an unforgivable sin to return them to the Jewish "sinners," who were still not prepared to be saved by accepting the

Christian redeemer. This religious belief made it extremely difficult for us to locate Jewish children who had been sheltered by the Lithuanian Christians.

After liberation, our first task was to seek out those children, sparing no effort to win them back to the faith of their parents. Nor did we hesitate to pay bribes where needed in order to save the relatively few surviving children.

I personally set out to save my little brothers and sisters who, in many cases, did not even know they were Jewish. Despite the danger of traveling — many gentiles were thrilled to shed the blood of a Jew — I traveled from town to town and from city to city to see if I could restore some of these lost little Jews to the Jewish people. More than once I heard the Lithuanians expressing shock, "Look! Am I seeing things? Isn't that a Jew? How come he wasn't exterminated by the Germans? He must have been hiding in Russia the whole time."

Brokenhearted, dispirited, I continued on my journey. Wherever I stopped, I immediately questioned gentiles if they knew or had heard tell of any Jewish children in the area. Told yes, I would hasten to check the facts. And if the report proved true, I would gird my loins and do everything I could to save the child. I was, thank G-d, often successful, and brought many children back to the tradition of their forefathers.

In the course of my travels, I came to the town of Zasli. There I was told that a Jewish girl was living in a nearby hamlet. I rushed there and found the teenaged girl among the non-Jews. She told me that she was from Kovno. I had known her family, respectable in scholarship and wealth. She told me her story of suffering and how she had been rescued during the seige of Kovno by the son of the gentile concierge of their house.

I asked her why she had not returned to live among Jews, since the danger to her had passed with the downfall of the accursed Germans. Bursting into tears, she confessed that the young gentile had taken advantage of her feelings of gratitude. She had borne a child who — in her words — was definitely a gentile because the father, who by then had left her and gone off to live somewhere in Germany, was a *goy[1]*. Since she loved her child, she did not wish to leave him among the gentiles. Convinced that the Jews would not accept her child as Jewish, she thought herself compelled to spend the rest of her life among the gentiles even though she truly wished to return to her people.

I asked her who had told her that her child was definitely a gentile. She answered, "That's what I thought. But if the rabbi agrees to circumcise my child and make a *pidyon haben[2]* for him, I'd be very happy to leave this village and return to live among my Jewish brothers and sisters."

I promised to do exactly what she asked for: her child would be accepted into the covenant of our forefather Abraham, he would be redeemed from the sanctity of a firstborn, and he would, G-d willing, be accepted as a full-fledged Jew, physically and spiritually.

But what indeed is the law regarding a child like this?

Response: According to Jewish law, this child is a kosher Jew and does not require any conversion. This is the opinion of the vast majority of Jewish authorities. But in order to satisfy the opinion of the minority who maintain that the child of a non-Jewish father and a Jewish mother is not a Jew, I had him immersed in a *mikveh.[3]*

During the circumcision, I told the *sandak[4]* to recite the blessing, *"Asher kideshonu bemitzvosov vetzivonu lehachniso biveriso shel Avrohom Ovinu."[5]* I also gave instructions that after the blessing everyone should respond, "Just as he has been inducted into the covenant, so may he be inducted into the study of Torah, go on to marry, and produce good deeds."

---

1. A non-Jew.
2. Redemption ceremony for a firstborn son in fulfilment of *Numbers* 18:15 and 16.
3. A ritual pool of water that meets extremely stringent requirements.
4. The man who holds the baby.
5. "Who has sanctified us by His commandments and has commanded us to induct him into the covenant of our Father Abraham.

In the prayer that is recited after the circumcision, I instructed that the words, "Maintain this child for his mother," be said but that no mention of the non-Jewish father be made. Similarly, the phrase, "Let the father rejoice," was skipped.

Usually the redemption of a firstborn son is performed by the father. Where the father is not alive, one either waits for the child to grow up and redeem himself or the court can step in and arrange for the redemption. In this case, where the father was not a Jew, it was possible that the child, upon reaching adulthood, would not redeem himself; that was one reason for the rabbinical court to step in. Furthermore, since redemption was one of the mother's stipulations for agreeing to return with me, we allowed the court to redeem this child. A feast was prepared and the child was redeemed by the court according to Halacha.[6] I took it upon myself to have this boy informed upon reaching adulthood that he is to redeem himself in order to satisfy the opinions of all the authorities.

The mother married an Orthodox Jew, and today her son studies in a yeshiva in the Holy Land. He is a fine scholar and, with G-d's help, will grow into a true Jewish leader.

6. Jewish Law.

97: *A Marrried Woman Who Bore a Gentile's Child*

Question: When I was working at rescuing Jewish children who had been living among the gentiles, a typically unfortunate situation was brought to my attention.

Rescuing Jewish children was fraught with the risks of traveling on dangerous roads and with the difficulties one faced upon discovering that the children he was looking for were in the hands of uncooperative non-Jews. It was essential to locate and remove every Jewish child as quickly as possible. More than once the gentiles found out that someone was coming to fetch the children, and by the time we arrived, the gentiles — who considered it a major theological achievement to save a Jewish soul — had hidden the child in some secret place and proceeded to deny the child's existence. They used any means to avoid returning these Jewish children to Jews.

Especially adept at this deceit were the priests and nuns who wanted to keep their grip on as many Jewish children as possible. They would admit piously that it was imperative that the children be returned to the Jews, while they simultaneously aided the gentiles who had hidden the children, doing everything in their power to prevent their return.

I therefore found it extraordinary when a gentile woman came and told me that she had attempted to return to his Jewish relatives a boy who had been placed in her care by his mother. But these relatives had refused to accept the child! I asked her for the entire story.

The child's mother was a Jewess who had died a short while before the liberation, and the father was a gentile who had hidden the Jewess from the Germans. Shortly before her death, she had asked this gentile woman for a promise that immediately after the war she would return her child to relatives of her husband from whom she had been forcibly separated before the persecutions.

The promise given, the mother had died in peace. Right after the war, the gentile woman had made every effort and succeeded in locating a relative of the child. To her great dismay, he had refused to take the child, claiming that the boy was not a Jew since his father was a gentile. Not knowing what else to do, she had decided to adopt the child herself and raise him as a gentile. Sometime later, the child's mother had come to her in a dream wailing bitterly and had begged her to go to a Jewish rabbi and tell him the whole story of the child as well as of the relative's refusal to raise the child. That was how she had come to me.

I thanked the gentile woman for her troubles and efforts, and then sent for the relative to hear his side of the story. The man, substantiating the woman's story, explained why he had sent the woman and the child away: The dead woman's husband, his relative, had survived the war and was living and practicing medicine in Minsk. When the woman had offered to return the child, he had immediately informed his relative, but since the child was the fruit of his wife's relationship with a non-Jew, the husband had not been interested in the child. The relative believed that the husband was right and that the child, the product of an adulterous union, would bring shame to the family's reputation. A *mamzer*[1], he would never be allowed to marry a Jewess. Since the husband had refused the child, the relative felt it was better for the boy to be raised by the gentile woman as a gentile instead of him or some other Jew adopting a *mamzer* who could never be integrated with the Jewish people.

---

1. The child of a union prohibited in *Leviticus* 18 for which the penalty listed in *Leviticus* 20 is either death or excision, with the sole exception of *nida*, is called a *mamzer* and is limited by *Deuteronomy* 23:3 to marrying another *mamzer* or a convert.

Response: I explained to the man that his assumption and subsequent behavior had been wrong. He had almost caused a Jewish soul to be lost to the Jewish people. The child was not only not a *mamzer*, but a full-fledged Jew. Only divine intervention had led the gentile woman to make such a scrupulous effort to fulfill her Jewish friend's last wish to perpetuate her family which had been exterminated by the German murderers. Were it not for her efforts, that boy would have become assimilated without ever learning his origins or the fate of his forefathers.

I told the relative that he was obligated to take back the child from the gentile woman. If he still felt that he could not raise the child, I would make arrangements to have him raised by a religious family.

The man accepted the proposal. After the formal arrangements to accept back the child from the gentile woman, I located an Orthodox family willing to adopt him. They eventually moved to London where the boy now studies in a yeshiva and is doing very well in his character development, much to the joy of his adoptive parents who love him as if he were their own flesh and blood.

The *halacha*[2] as to whether such a child is a *mamzer* or not can be summed up as follows: The child of such a union is kosher even though the mother was married. His not being a *mamzer* is unequivocal, and I ruled that he be circumcised in accord with Torah law. Nevertheless, to satisfy the opinion of a minority of codifiers that the child of a non-Jewish father and a Jewish mother is considered a non-Jew and requires conversion, I ruled that he be immersed in a *mikveh* .

2. Ruling in Jewish Law.

3. A ritual pool of water that meets extremely stringent requirements.

98: *The Case of the Mamzer[1] Rabbi*

Question: Were all the oceans ink and all the skies parchment, and every single person on earth a scribe, they could never relate in its entirety all that our enemies — the accursed Germans — did to the Jewish people. Only G-d in heaven knows what the Jews suffered. Even today our wounds still bleed. The taunting voices of the blasphemers saying, "Where is your G-d?" still grate in our ears.

The roots of the following problem lie in those days of torture and brutality, but the problem itself surfaced years later in another country to the great sorrow of all involved. On 12 Tishrey 5702 — October 3, 1941 — the ghetto prisoners heard of a morbid edict — morbid even by German standards. The Germans murderers had decided that since there were more women than men in the ghetto as a result of the previous *Akzionen* (forays) in which more men had been killed than women, they would equalize the numbers by putting all unmarried women to death. Only women who had husbands to support them would be left alive.

It was only a rumor, but as a result all the single women in the ghetto, in order to save themselves from certain death, began to scurry around for husbands. They took anyone willing to marry them; they were happy to be married at all. One woman, who had lost all trace of her husband when he was taken away by the accursed Germans, assumed he was

1. The child of a union prohibited in *Leviticus* 18 for which the penalty listed in *Leviticus* 20 is either death or excision, with the sole exception of *nida*, is called a *mamzer* and is limited by *Deuteronomy* 23:3 to marrying another *mamzer* or a convert.

dead. Fearing for her life, she found a man and married him. Together they managed to escape from the ghetto, surviving the war in a hideout.

When the war ended, they traveled to another country and, like so many other Jews, struggled to put down new roots. They were blessed with a son who studied Torah in a yeshiva. His love for Judaism was strong, and he eventually became the rabbi of a Jewish community.

One day this young rabbi's world suddenly turned dark. A man appeared and exploded the news that he was the first husband of the rabbi's mother, the husband long presumed dead. He explained that although the Germans had taken him away and detained him for a long time, he had survived. Immediately after liberation, he had begun to search for his wife, and had been seeking her ever since. When he found out that she had married another man and had borne him a son, he was furious at his wife's betrayal. He decided to track her down, force her to divorce her second husband and publicly reveal her shame. Even more, he wanted to make sure that her son, a *mamzer*, the product of this adulterous marriage, should never be able to live among Jews.

But in the meantime his wife had died, and all his vengefulness was directed at the son, the *mamzer* rabbi: His career would be destroyed, he would have to divorce his wife, and his children would be declared *mamzerim*.

This young rabbi, a genuinely religious Jew, fainted when he heard the bitter tale of his birth. When he came to, he bewailed his fate. Besides his own suffering, he was most upset at the desecration of G-d that would result when the public found out that the rabbi of their community was a *mamzer* and forbidden to marry most Jewesses. He begged his mother's first husband not to publicize the matter immediately but to wait until he could consult with Jewish scholars to determine what ought to be done to prevent public desecration of G-d.

When the young rabbi came to me, I was shocked to see him so devastated. He was bent over like an old man, and gray hairs had begun to sprout in his beard and on his head.

With gushing tears, he told me the story and asked me to tell him what must happen to him, his family, and his community according to the laws of the Torah.

Response: According to Halacha a *mamzer* is fit to be a rabbi or a judge. He may rule on the permissible and the forbidden as well as handle court cases. That young rabbi was permitted to remain the rabbi and spiritual leader of his community even though he was a *mamzer*. The only remaining issue was *chilul HaShem*, desecration of G-d.

Chasam Sofer (*Even HaEzer* 2:94) writes, "Even though a *mamzer* who is a Torah scholar is to be honored in every way, he is not be appointed as rabbi of a community because people will not listen to him. 'Go see what your mother has done,' they will say. In our generation, in which due respect is not given to the Torah, this is even more true. Even the most respected rabbis of impeccable lineage are subjected to indignities. There is no reason [for a man] to hold on to the position of rabbi if the community will not honor him properly."

So I ruled that this young rabbi should resign. I also made the necessary arrangements for him to divorce his wife, for the Halacha forbids a *mamzer* to be married to a Jewish-born woman unless she is also a *mamzeress*. I also called in his mother's first husband and tried to persuade him not to publicize the matter because it would cause *chilul HaShem*. He had already achieved the destruction of the rabbi's family, his career, and his spiritual life. What could he gain by shaming him in public except the shedding of more blood? The son was certainly not responsible for his mother's actions; until the man came along, he had known nothing about his origins.

99: *Women Prostituted by the Germans*

Question: Immediately after our liberation from the ghetto, a horrifying problem was brought to my attention. It applied not only to the woman who posed it to me but to a large sisterhood of Jewish women who had suffered abominably during the Holocaust years.

A young woman from a respected family in Kovno came to me with tears gushing down her cheeks. She, like many of her unfortunate sisters, had been captured by the accursed Germans and forced into prostitution. The evildoers had not only made free use of her pure body, but had also tattooed the words "prostitute for Hitler's soldiers" on her.

After the liberation she was reunited with her husband who had also survived. Their children had been killed by the Germans, and they hoped to establish a new family on the basis of Jewish sanctity and purity. But when her husband saw the words on her body he was extremely upset, and decided they must clarify first whether he was allowed to live with her according to Halacha, for if she had even once willingly slept with a German she might be forbidden to her husband.

Response: I ruled that this unfortunate woman and all her sisterhood who were so shamed might return to their husbands and live with them as man and wife. The only exception would be when the husband is a *kohein*[1] in which case, even though she had been raped, he would be forbidden to live with her. But where the husband is not a *kohein* there

1. Every descendant of Aaron, the brother of Moses, is a *Kohein* (plural, *Kohanim*).

is absolutely no reason to forbid the woman to her husband.

G-d forbid that we speak evil of these kosher Jewish women. On the contrary, it is a mitzva to publicize the great reward that they will receive from Him Who hears the entreaties of the suffering. He will certainly cure their broken hearts, heal them emotionally, and grant them His blessings. We must prevent any additional suffering by these women, as was the case with a number of them, whose husbands divorced them. Woe unto us that this should have happened in our times!

I ruled that there was no need for her to try to have the tattoo obliterated. On the contrary, let her and her sisters preserve their tattoos and regard them not as signs of shame, but as signs of honor, pride, and courage — proof of what they suffered for the sanctification of G-d. The inscription the murderers used to defile and shame these pure Jewish women is an honor for them and for our people. We shall yet live to see the corpses and the eternal shame of those evildoers. These inscriptions will constantly remind us of the verse in the Torah of Moshe, "Nations, praise His people! For He will avenge the blood of His servants and return vengeance upon His enemies."

100: *Removing Numbers Branded by the Germans on Their Victims*

Question: After the liberation, a young woman from a respected family asked me the following question. Since the accursed Germans had branded her with a number in accord with their system of assigning numbers to every prisoner in the concentration camp, she wanted to have plastic surgery performed to remove the mark which constantly reminded her of the horor of those years. According to Halacha, is it permissible to remove the number?

Response: The accursed Germans branded these numbers on the arms of Jews as a sign of shame, as though to say that the bearers of these branded numbers are not human beings, but cattle to be brutally beaten, tortured, and slaughtered at will.

Not only should these numbers not denigrate us but, on the contrary, such a number should be viewed as a sign of honor and glory, as a monument to the unforgivable bestiality of those vile murderers. As part of the plot to exterminate the holy seed of Jacob, leaving neither seed nor scion of the Jewish people, the branded numbers guaranteed that if a Jew ever escaped from a camp, the imprint on his arm would reveal to everyone who found him that he was a Jew and fair game to be put to death. This horrifying number is a sign whereby the German heinousness is remembered. G-d forbid that we ever forget what those evil people did to us.

The obligation to recall the entire scope of German wickedness, not taking our minds off it for even a moment, is today a redoubled obligation. See how the accursed Germans spare no effort to mislead the world into forgetting the evils that they perpetrated. So long as the blood of our martyred

195

brothers and sisters cries out to us from the earth and demands vengeance, this sign branded on the arms of the survivors serves as a reminder that declares, "Let it be known among the nations before our eyes — the vengeance that You will pay for the blood of Your servants that was shed. For You, the seeker of blood, will recall them, You have not forgotten. the cry of the humble." Raise up Your Jewish people, the nation so denigrated and oppressed, raise them up again among the nations as in the past.

I feel that this woman should under no circumstances remove the branded number from her arm, for by doing so she is fulfilling the wishes of the accursed German evildoers and abetting their effort to have the Holocaust forgotten, as if we Jews had created a fiction against them. Let her wear the sign with pride.

101: *The Cross on The Biceps*

Question: The accursed murderers used to take Jews out to slave labor in the middle of the night, allowing them no opportunity to don *tefilin*[1] before going off to work. They used to force us to work throughout the entire day till late at night.

Some slave laborers dared don *tefilin* secretly as day broke while walking to work. The Germans on one occasion caught one of these slave laborers with his *tefilin* on. After torturing him at great length, they decided to carve a cross on his left biceps so that he could not bare his arm for *tefilin* without people seeing the sign of shame that the accursed evildoers had emblazoned on his flesh. I was asked after liberation whether it was permissible for him to put a bandage over the wound and don *tefilin* over the bandage, for the bandage would give people the impression that he had a wound on his biceps. Since *tefilin* must normally be worn directly on the flesh, would this bandage be considered interference, or not?

Response: I ruled that the man should don both the arm and the head *tefilin* at home before going to the synagogue to pray, so that no one should see the cross on his biceps. After prayer he could remove the head *tefilin* in the synagogue and the arm *tefilin* at home.

Should he find this difficult to do, I allowed him to don the arm *tefilin* over a thin shirt sleeve. But if he chose to do that he was not to recite a *beracha*[2] upon donning the arm *tefilin*, but was to recite both *berachos* when donning the head *tefilin*.

1. *Tefilin*, phylacteries, are worn on one's head and arm in fulfilment of *Exodus* 13: 9 and 16, and *Deuteronomy* 6: 8 and 11: 18.
2. The blessing recited upon performing a *mitzva*.

197

102: *People Who Lived as Gentiles and Are Now Returning to the Jewish Fold*

Question: In the days when the German murderers were busy annihilating the Jewish people, there were Jews who disguised themselves as gentiles so that the murderers would not recognize them and murder them. They acted as good Christians, attended church, wore crosses around their necks, and his every indication that they were Jewish.

Later, when G-d arose to judge the earth and the murderers' might was destroyed, those Jews who had been swallowed up among the gentiles felt that it was time to rejoin their people. And the question was asked whether they ought to be received without any difficulty at all, or whether special requirements of *teshuva*, of repentance, should be demanded.

Response: The gentiles neither compelled one to attend church nor to wear a cross around his neck. Whoever did that did so willingly and deliberately in order to save himself from being annihilated with the rest of the Jewish people. It seems that he ought not to be accepted by the rest of the Jewish people without some genuine signs of penitence.

103: *May One Who Disguised Himself As a Catholic Correct Torah Scrolls?*

Question: When the liberation took place and we were freed from the yoke of the abominable Germans, it was very difficult to find an expert scribe who could repair a Torah scroll or a pair of *tefilin*[1] and make it again kosher. Most of the scribes had been among the martyred. I was asked the following question. Among the liberated Jews there was one scribe who knew the laws of writing, examination, and repair perfectly. However, much to our sorrow, everyone knew that during the war years he had disguised himself as a non-Jew, had worn a cross around his neck, and had bought himself a baptismal certificate. To save his life and protect himself from being arrested by the Germans or handed over by the Lithuanians for blood money, he had attended church like the most devout Catholic. Might he now return to his profession, the sanctified labor of repairing Torah-scrolls, *tefilin,* and *mezuzos*[2]?

Response: The man may return to his craft as a scribe and he is allowed to repair Torah-scrolls, *tefilin*, and *mezuzos*. One consideration is that this immediate post-war period is one of dire spiritual need and there is no one else who can inspect and correct for us. And the fact that the man had disguised himself as a Catholic during the war years cannot be held against him for he did so out of compulsion to save his life.

1. *Tefillin,* phylacteries, are worn on one's head and arm in fulfilment of *Exodus* 13: 9 and 16, and *Deuteronomy* 6: 8 and 11: 18.

2. *Mezuzos* (singular, *Mezuza)* are parchment scrolls containing two paragraphs from *Deuteronomy,* 6: 4-9 and 11: 13-21. which are attached to the doorposts of a Jew's home.

That he did not don *tefilin* during those years is not enough to disqualify him, because he was afraid of being recognized as a Jew. Now, after the liberation, we see that he is an observant Jew again in every respect, and that his repentance is complete. He even accepts insults silently. We cannot deny him the right to serve as a scribe because of what he did to save his life, especially now that we are in need of his services as a result of the Russian domination of Lithuania.

•

104: *A Jew Who Defended Murderers of Jews*

Question: After the German armies retreated from Lithuania, two Lithuanian murderers of some 20 Jews were captured in Kaidan. The two hired a Jewish lawyer for a great sum of money — money they had looted from Jews — to defend them.

The Jews in town begged this lawyer not to defend those murderers. But their requests were in vain. Understandably, the local Jews regarded the lawyer as an outcast and refused to have any dealings with him.

One day, on the *yahrzeit*[1] of one of his parents, the lawyer came to the synagogue known as Hoisman's Kloiz to pray and say Kaddish[2]; of all the synagogues Kovno had once had, this was the only one left. The man stepped up to the *amud*[3] to lead the prayers, shocking the people by his shameless audacity. Not only had he ignored their simple request not to defend the Lithuanian murderers for Jewish blood money, but he dared enter a holy synagogue, knowing that all his Jewish brethren considered him defiled, an outcast, and then dared grab the *amud* in an attempt to act as the emissary of this congregation before G-d.

Reuven the sexton was so shaken when he saw the lawyer step forward to lead the prayers that he rushed over to the man, pushed him away from the *amud*, and yelled out, "Abominable one! Step out of this holy place! Don't you dare

---

1. Anniversary of death.
2. A prayer for the dead recited during public prayer sessions.
3. Lectern.

set foot in the synagogue again!" All the worshipers present stepped into the next room to pray, leaving the lawyer alone in the synagogue in tears.

I was asked whether Reuven the sexton's action was in accord with Halacha and whether the men who stepped into the next room had acted correctly according to Halacha. Perhaps they should have let him commemorate the *yahrzeit,* and should not have insulted him by pushing him away?

Response: The major code of Jewish law[4] reads, "A communal emissary must be a suitable person. What constitutes 'suitable'? That he be free of sin and never have had a bad reputation, not even in his youth, and that he be humble and pleasing to the public."

Clearly, a man willing to defend murderers for money, ignoring the request of his Jewish brethren not to do so, was not a suitable emissary. What greater sin can there be than protecting murderers from being punished? Should the lawyer proceed with the case and win it, the murderers would have thought that there is neither law nor judge in the world. One must even consider that at the first opportunity those abominable murderers would rob and murder Jews again.

That lawyer, in accepting the case of those Lithuanian murderers, had acted contrary to Halacha. Even if the murderers had been Jews being brought to trial in a non-Jewish court, they were not to be bailed out. We rejoice when a murderer is brought to justice; for if we had the authority, we ourselves would sentence him to death.

Reuven the sexton acted properly when he pushed the man away from the *amud,* and the men were right in stepping out of the synagogue. They thus protested Jews' defending murderers who had shed blood without a drop of mercy for young or old.

Accompanied by several other men, I visited the lawyer in his office and spoke with him at length, asking him to withdraw from the case. I explained the great desecration of

4. *Shulchan Aruch Orach Chayim* 53:4.

G-d involved if he appeared in court as a defender of the Lithuanian murderers. The reaction of the gentiles would be, "Jews are ready to do anything for money," as his own actions were proving. Not only was he defending murderers who might very well have butchered his own relatives, but the payment for their defense was tainted with Jewish blood, for it was money that the murderers had looted from their Jewish victims.

Thank G-d, my words penetrated the lawyer's heart. He resigned from the case and began to pray with us every day. Sometime later he left Kovno for fear that the murderers might avenge themselves upon him.

It is common knowledge that many of the murderers assumed new identities and escaped to foreign countries, pretending that they had never touched a Jew, while their hands were drenched with blood. It is a great mitzva to do everything in one's power to expose these murderers and to bring them to justice. It is certainly forbidden to help them avoid the just retribution due them for their crimes.

105: *Penance for Owning a Passport Identifying Oneself as a Catholic*

Question: After the liberation, Mr. S.A. came to me with a serious question. During the days of evil and atrocity, he had found a hideout for himself and his family in a gentile home. To insure that the accursed Germans would not discover their secret in the course of one of their frequent searches for hidden Jews, he purchased false documents which identified him and his family as born Catholics. He thanked G-d that the need to use them had never arisen.

But what worried him was whether or not the very possession of those documents constituted a denial of his Jewish faith, turning him into an apostate. Was he obligated to immerse himself in a *mikveh*[1] and to accept upon himself specific penance?

On the other hand, he had never actually used those documents and, throughout the years of evil, had never committed any act of apostasy, neither in word nor in action. In the hideout he had lived as a kosher Jew, donning *tefilin*[2] daily, keeping the Sabbath, and being careful to avoid eating non-kosher food. Therefore, he might not be obligated to immerse himself in a *mikveh* or to do any special penance.

Response: The purchase of these identity documents to be used in case he was ever caught by the accursed Germans did not constitute an act of apostasy performed in public, because under no circumstances were ten Jews aware of his situation. His only sin was thinking of using them; but none of his actions constituted a desecration of G-d.

1. A ritual pool of water that meets extremely stringent requirements.
2. *Tefilin,* phylacteries, are worn on one's head and arm in fulfilment of *Exodus* 13: 9 and 16, and *Deuteronomy* 6: 8 and 11: 18.

Since he was kept alive by the grace of G-d and never had to use the documents, and considering the fact that throughout the entire period of his hiding he acted Jewishly in every respect, I believed that a lenient ruling was called for. I ruled that he did not require immersion or acceptance of any penance as if he had been an apostate, G-d forbid.

106: *The Repentant Kapo*[1]

Question: My soul weeps when I recall how the German evildoers deceived the Jewish people and blasphemed G-d. As a result of their evil, another evil was born: Jewish Kapos. Serving the Germans, they yelled and beat and informed against their fellow-Jews, making their lives miserable.

When the enemy was finally crushed and the day of reckoning come at last, our suffering brothers within the confines of the ghetto walls burst out into the open spaces, and bit by bit began to restore the pieces of their lives. They praised the One Above for finally redeeming His people from their torturers. The houses of worship filled up, and once again the prayers of Jacob and the hum of Torah could be heard.

That was when I was asked about one of the Jewish policemen. Claiming that he regretted his actions and had repented fully for his evil deeds, he sought to be appointed a cantor and to lead the prayers before Him Who heeds the prayers of the Jewish people. Would this be appropriate?

Response: I ruled that this man was not to be appointed a cantor. All the sources of Halacha indicate that a man should not be appointed to any communal position if he has or had a reputation as a sinner. This was certainly true for this man; everyone knew how he had cursed and beaten his fellow-Jews. No matter how much penance he might claim to have done, he was not be appointed to any communal position.

1. Acronym for *Katzetpolizei* — camp police

107: *A Kapo's[1] Name*

Question: A unique place in the history of the holocaust is occupied by Jews who, either freely or under orders, served the accursed Germans, hoping that their cooperation would spare them the fate of their brothers and sisters. But in the end, it merely delayed their death. Most of them were forced to do the Germans' work against their will; others naively thought that they might exploit their positions to help their brethren. But whoever got friendly with the Germans, for whatever reason, was loathed by his fellow-Jews and considered a traitor.

One man who had served the Germans as a Kapo was about to be put to death. In the presence of his fellow-Jews he bemoaned his sins, cried bitter tears, and begged forgiveness from his Creator for his evil deeds.

Since it is the custom to call a man up to the Torah with the announcement, "Let So-and-so son of So-and-so rise," the question was asked if this Kapo's name might be uttered when his son was called up to the Torah? Or was the name of an evildoer never to be mentioned as King Solomon said in *Proverbs*, "Let the name of the wicked rot."

Response: Since the man repented before dying, I ruled that his name should be mentioned. Besides, we must consider the son's feelings. Why should the son, an observant Jew, not be allowed to mention his father's name?

Moreover, since the man was martyred by the Germans, his death served as atonement for his sins. Let his name be mentioned when his son performs this mitzva in order to provide merit for the father in the World of Reward.

---

1. Acronym for *Katzetpolizei* — camp police

108: *A Kohein¹ Who Converted to Christianity*

Question: During the days of the Second World War darkness, when our nation was victimized by the Germans, our brethren were butchered, burnt, and cremated, and many lost hope of ever surviving. Some, seeking any way to stay alive, even accepted baptismal waters, and denied their origins and the covenant of their forefathers.

After the evildoers lost the war, the lost souls who had assimilated among the gentiles began to taste the dew of redemption, and felt that it was time to seek ways to return to their origins and rejoin the Jewish people.

A Jewish soldier in the Russian army told me about a husband and wife imprisoned with German prisoners of war in a POW camp who claimed to be Jewish even though they had been baptized. Now they wanted to return to their Jewish brethren. Eventually, the couple managed to leave the prisoner-of-war camp and settle in Kovno. The man used to come and pray in the *beis hamidrash²* every morning and evening. A question arose: since the man was a *kohein*, might he raise his hands to bless the congregation?

Response: The fact that the *kohein* had undergone baptism was immaterial, for he had acted only under the greatest of duress, fearing for his life. That had been a clear act of compulsion of which the man repented completely without any attempt at deception. He prayed genuinely, morning

---

1. Every descendant of Aaron, the brother of Moses, is a *Kohein* (plural, *Kohanim)*.

2. House of Study.

and evening. Furthermore, he wished to go up with the other *kohanim* to fulfill the commandment of blessing the Jewish people. I ruled that it was permissible for him to raise his hands in blessing.

But there was another, more serious problem: A *kohein* who converted and then rejoined the Jewish people may face a problem if his wife was baptized before he married her. Her conversion prior to marriage puts her according to Halacha in the category of a *zona* who may not marry a *kohein*. Their children, in turn, are considered *chalalim*, and their daughters are forbidden to marry *kohanim*. I therefore sought testimony from dependable witnesses as to whether they had been married before their baptism.

Another issue was that they had not immediately rejoined the Jewish people after the liberation, flawing their repentance. But this objection was not material, because it was quite possible that in their terror they had not been aware that it was safe to return to Jewish observance. Besides, the man did not believe that there were still Jews in Kovno to return to; it took a while for that knowledge to penetrate. I instructed them to immerse in a *mikveh*[3] in accord with the Halachic requirement for any Jew who leaves his faith and returns to it.

---

3. A ritual pool of water that meets very stringent requirements.

109: *Burying a Possible Apostate*

Question: After the city of Kovno was liberated from the accursed Germans — may their name be obliterated — we emerged from our hiding places in cellars and caves, alive despite the enemy's desire to eliminate the word "Jew" forever. One of the first things we were faced with were the remains of martyrs whose bodies lay abandoned in the streets and fields like ordinary fertilizer one avoided stepping on. It was a nightmare. Everywhere we looked we saw skeletons and single limbs, skulls and bones. The most wretched scene was inside the concentration camp known as the Kovno Katzetlager. Nothing remained except the empty shells of huts which the Germans had burned to the ground in order to rout any Jews hiding underneath the structures. Scorched bones and human hands could be seen protruding from these piles of ashes. We made every effort to bury those sacred bones, and to offer the remains of our brothers and sisters the final courtesy. We searched for additional bones everywhere, especially inside the ruins of the buildings that had been knows as Blocks A, B, and C, where a great number of Jews had lived.

It is hard to set down in writing the pathetic and horrible sights we saw while we collected these remains. Among the bodies we found the remains of a woman holding two infants in her arms. The hand that writes these words trembles and from the depths of the heart bursts forth a cry, "Why, O G-d, have you done this to us? Why did you hand us over like sheep to the slaughter?"

We also found the body of a man in whose pocket was a small *mezuza*[1] case with a scrap of paper on which was written "Yisroel ben Paltiel of Berlin." This and the fact that he was circumcised indicated that the man had been Jewish. But there was a surprising contradiction: around his neck hung a chain with a cross on it. The question then arose as to the proper way to treat this body. Were we to treat him like another Jew or like an apostate? Were we obligated to provide burial for him? Might we bury him among Jews? Or were we to bury him outside the cemetery, away from the graves of our sacred martyrs?

Response: We were definitely obligated to bury this corpse, even if the man was an apostate. There was no reason to doubt that the man was a Jew. His circumcision, as well as the scrap of paper with the name on it — it was very reasonable to assume that it was his own name — proved that. And the probable reason for the cross around the neck was that he had hoped, in vain, that it might save his life from the hands of the blood thirsty hordes.

Nevertheless I ruled that he should not be buried near other martyrs. We never bury the wicked alongside the righteous nor do we bury a very wicked man near a less wicked one. We bury kind next to kind. Since a possibility existed that this Jew had been an apostate, he was not to be buried alongside the martyrs.

---

1. *Mezuzos* (singular, *mezuza)* are parchment scrolls containing two paragraphs from *Deuteronomy,* 6: 4-9 and 11: 13-21, which are attached to the doorposts of a Jew's home.

110: *May a Mercy Killer Lead Prayers?*

Question: One ice-cold winter day, the slave laborers were being beaten by their accursed oppressors to move more quickly. But they could not. Dressed in the poorest of rags that barely covered them, let alone provided any warmth, the unfortunate and miserable Jews were suffering from horrible pain. Their feet had swollen from the great cold. Every step was torture. From time to time they stumbled. Many of those who fell never rose again.

After seeing scores of his fellow-prisoners fall and die on the spot, one of these marchers, unable to walk any longer because of his own unbearable suffering, said to his friend struggling right behind him, "Please do me a favor. Give me a push so that I will fall. If I rise, push me down again. And again. Eventually my strength will give out and I will not be able to rise again. I cannot bear the pain and the suffering. I prefer to be dead."

Unable to convince his stronger friend to carry out this act, he had to beg him again and again. Finally the man took pity on the broken Jew, saying to himself, "What difference does it make if he dies now or later? He is better off dead than living in so much pain. Since he begs me with the last ounce of strength, how can I not do what he asks?"

So the friend pushed him down and, when he rose up again, he pushed him down again. Although the man was able to get up each time, when he got to his place of work he was so weak that he simply collapsed and died.

After our liberation in 1944, when we were blessed by G-d to see the end of the power of the wicked Germans, we began to arrange the High Holy Days prayers. As is customary in

212

Jewish communities, we sought a man who would meet all the requirements for leading the prayer on such awesome and holy days. After an exhaustive search, we found a suitable man. But a number of people identified him as the man who had pushed his friend to death. They claimed that a murderer was unfit to lead our prayers on Rosh Hashana and Yom Kipur. The questions I had to answer were the following: Was the man considered a murderer? Did he have to accept special penance — generally a personalized program of self-denial, study, and sometimes affliction — for his sin? And would the penance suffice to allow him to lead the public prayers?

Since it was difficult to find a suitable replacement and time was extremely short, I was asked to seek some way, in accord with the law of the Torah, to permit him to lead the prayers for the surviving Jews.

Response: The man who pushed his friend is not to be regarded as an outright murderer but rather as someone who brought about the death of a fellow-Jew. For the victim did not die immediately after being pushed, but rather continued to walk until he reached his place of work where he finally collapsed and died. In fact, there is no evidence that he died as a result of being pushed; it may very well be that he would have died anyway. To atone, it is enough that he do penance.

But the penance should be severe, because Maimonides does consider a man who brings about the death of another a murderer. Even though he may be innocent in the eyes of the Torah, it cannot be forgotten that he brought about the death of his fellow-Jew. He must therefore accept upon himself full penance, and only after he carries it out may he lead the community in prayer. I also instructed him, after the penance, to immerse himself in a *mikveh*[1] as part of the purification process, after which G-d would erase his sins and heed his prayers.

1. A ritual pool of water that meets extremely stringent requirements.

After the man had carried out the entire sequence of penance, he led the prayers on the High Holy Days with deep emotion, sighing and weeping. Many Jewish Russian soldiers from the front joined us, and they too were greatly inspired and stirred by this man's sincere, broken-hearted cries.

111: *A Kohein¹ Who Killed A Gentile*

Question: After the liberation, people began to return to their hometowns to seek out relatives and any clues as to their fate; they also sought to salvage what they could of their possessions.

Among the Jews who had been exiled to Russia and then returned to Kovno, there was a man who used to come to pray with our *minyon²* every morning and every evening in the *beis hamidrosh³* that we had in Hoisman's Kloiz on 28 Morani Street. He also used to join the students of the daily Talmud *Daf Yomi⁴* class I taught at the time.

The man was very observant, precise in his attention to the details of mitzvos⁵, and acted the way a true lover and seeker of G-d behaves. He was charitable, generous, and well-liked by everyone. As a *kohein*, he would go up to bless the community on holidays, and the people were enchanted by a special melody he used during the blessing.

During one of the holidays, a man who had just returned to Kovno, came over to me and said, "Rabbi, this man should not be allowed to bless the public. I know that he killed someone. You must forbid him to raise his hands in blessing."

After the holiday I visited the *kohein* to hear his side of the story. This is what he told me:

1. Every descendant of Aaron, the brother of Moses, is a *Kohein* (plural, *Kohanim*).
2. Quorum.
3. House of study.
4. Leaf of Talmud studied throughout the world on a given day.
5. Commandments.

"I used to peddle merchandise from village to village through back roads and forests. I always carried a loaded revolver for self-protection. The widow of a poor man who had been murdered by a Lithuanian gentile came to me with the following request, 'You know my bitter situation, and that I am without any support. A Lithuanian broke into my house and robbed the last remnants of my property, removing my furniture and my utensils.'

" 'Tell me what I can do for you,' I said to her.

"She said, 'Please go and threaten the Lithuanian with your gun. Tell him to return the poor widow's property, and that if he refuses, you'll shoot him.'

"I felt that I might be able to help her. So I went to the Lithuanian's house, took out my revolver and set it down next to me on the table with its barrel pointing toward him. I attemped to intimidate him into returning her property to her. But the thief was unimpressed by my revolver; he showed no fear. In fact he got so angry that he tried to grab my revolver away and aim it at me.

"Naturally I resisted; my life was at stake. We wrestled, each of us trying to get his hand on the revolver and, in the course of our struggle, the gun went off and the bullet killed him. I still do not know how the trigger was pulled or who pulled it. I have no recollection of pulling the trigger since the revolver was not in my hand at all."

Response: I concluded that this death not be regarded as an accidental murder, but as manslaughter, for the *kohein* never intended to kill this gentile but only wished to intimidate him. Moreover, at the moment that he did kill the man, if indeed it was his finger on the trigger, he was in danger of his own life, for if the Lithuanian had taken control of the gun, he would have killed him. Even if the *kohein* had killed the man deliberately in the course of the fighting over the gun, he would not be liable since it had been done in self-defense.

Since the *kohein* regretted his action and accepted penance for having indirectly killed a man, all the views in

216

Halacha concur that he is allowed to raise his hands in priestly benediction. So I instructed him to pay no attention to any remarks made to him about the death of the gentile. Nor did the government ever find it necessary to place the man on trial for the gentile's death.

112: *Cannibalism*

Question: In 1977, there was a major news story about an airplane that crashed in the Andes Mountains of Chile where the few survivors waited more than 10 weeks in the 12,000 foot-high peaks until they were rescued. It was learned later that in order to survive, they were compelled to eat the flesh of their dead co-travelers. Mr. A. Goldstein asked me whether during the Holocaust, when Jews were starving in the ghettos and in the concentration camps, there was ever an incident where Jews ate the flesh of their fellow-Jews in order to survive. May a Jew eat the flesh of a dead human being in order to save his life?

Response: After studying the sources of Halacha on this subject I concluded that it is permissible to eat the flesh of a human corpse for survival. Nevertheless, I never heard of any instance of cannibalism in the Kovno Ghetto or in the nearby camps. What I do know is that next to the area where the Jewish slave laborers worked there was a prisoner-of-war-camp for Russian soldiers captured by the Germans. The Jewish laborers related to me that they saw the prisoners of war roasting the flesh of a dead soldier and eating it. A friend, who was in the Theresienstadt concentration camp, told me that he never saw or heard of Jewish cannibalism.

How glorious are the Jewish people! One cannot imagine, let alone describe, the hunger that raged in the concentration camps and the ghettoes among the Jews. Even so, the Jewish people did not descend from their level of sanctity; they never ate human flesh.

MOVING INTO THE GHETTO. Kovno was occupied by the Germans on June 24, 1941. On July 11, an order was issued to the effect that between July 15 and August 15, 1941, all the city's Jews were to move into a ghetto set up in Slobodka.

ENTRANCE TO THE GHETTO. The ghetto set up in Slobodka for the Jews of Kovno initially housed a population of almost 30,000. But of these, some 13,000 were murdered already during the first months of the ghetto's existence, mainly at the Seventh and Ninth Forts near Slobodka.

THE GHETTO BRIDGE. The Kovno ghetto was divided into two parts, the Big ghetto and the Little ghetto. The two ghettos were linked by a wooden bridge that was heavily guarded by Germans and Lithuanians.

JEWS AT THE SEVENTH FORT. Soon after the German occupation of Kovno, about 10,000 Jews were seized in various parts of the city and taken to the Seventh Fort, a part of the city's ancient fortifications. Between 6,000 and 7,000 of these Jews were murdered early in July 1941.

THE NINTH FORT near Slobodka, the end of the road for inmates of the Kovno ghetto and Jewish deportees from Germany, France and other Nazi-occupied countries. Jews imprisoned in the Ninth Fort were either murdered on the spot or sent on to death camps.

UMSIEDLUNGSAKTION (OPERATION RESETTLEMENT): Jews about to be deported from the Kovno ghetto. In two such *Aktionen* in 1942, Jews were transferred from the Kovno ghetto to the ghetto of Riga, Latvia. In October 1943, about 3,000 additional Jews were deported from the Kovno ghetto to concentration camps in Estonia.

LIFE IN THE KOVNO GHETTO. Jews with the Star of David plainly visible on their outer clothing.

LEADERS OF THE KOVNO GHETTO. The *Ältestenrat* (Council of Jewish Elders). Seated in the center is the chairman, Dr. Elhanan Elkes, a physician. After the liquidation of the ghetto, Dr. Elkes was deported to Dachau, where he died on July 25, 1944, a week before the liberation of Kovno.

THE GHETTO POLICE. The Jewish police force responsible for the maintenance of order in the Kovno ghetto under the supervision of the *Altestenrat* (Council of Jewish Elders). This police force helped some 250 armed Jewish fighters escape from the ghetto and join partisan units in the woods outside Kovno.

MUTUAL ASSISTANCE IN THE KOVNO GHETTO. Ghetto inmates reading an appeal for used clothing: "Jews! Donate for the poor and the naked — old winter clothing and shoes you no longer need! Do not stint! Give generously!"

COLLECTING "ARTIFACTS OF THE EXTINCT JEWISH RACE." Nazi postwar plans included exhibits of Jewish books and ceremonial objects as "artifacts of the extinct Jewish race." To this end, the Germans ordered the collection of all Jewish books in the ghettos, to be stored in warehouses until the exhibits could be organized. Here, ghetto children attempt to rescue books about to be carted off to the warehouse in the Kovno ghetto. Rabbi Oshry served for a time as custodian of this warehouse. This position gave him a unique opportunity to protect the books from desecration. Perhaps even more important, it afforded him access to major works of Rabbinic literature which he used as reference in the formulation of his *Teshuvot* (responsa) to questions on Jewish religious observances in the ghetto.

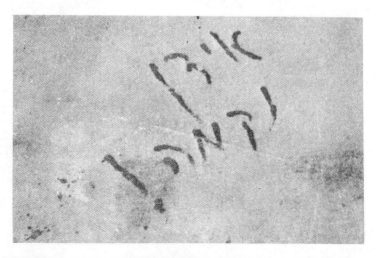

GRAFFITI ON A WALL IN THE KOVNO GHETTO. "Jews! Take Revenge!"

THE KOVNO GHETTO IN FLAMES. In July 1944, as Soviet forces approached Kovno, the Germans liquidated the ghetto, using grenades and explosives to kill Jews hiding in the ghetto's bunkers. About 8,000 Jews were sent from the ghetto to concentration camps in Germany proper. Over 80 percent of them died before the end of Hitler's Third Reich.

AFTER THE LIQUIDATION OF THE GHETTO. The bodies of Jews massacred during the liquidation of the Kovno ghetto in July 1944.

THE NINTH FORT. Piles of dead Jews placed on gasoline-soaked stacks of wood for cremation. Russian forces arrived in Kovno before the Germans could finish the cremation.

THE SURVIVORS. In front of the ghetto bunker in which he survived, an engineer, Indursky (left, front) explains to Red Army Major Bulganov (in uniform, at right) how the bunker was built. Rabbi Oshry (beardless, in dark jacket) is standing between Indursky and Major Bulganov.

AFTER LIBERATION. A group of partisans and Jewish survivors at the Ninth Fort, August, 1944. Rabbi Oshry (wearing a hat) is in the center.

THE AFTERMATH. German prisoners are forced to help bury the Jewish dead in the ghetto cemetary.

TRIBUTE TO THE DEAD. Rabbi Oshry (in tallith), flanked by Jewish partisans, eulogizes the martyrs of the ghetto on the grounds of the Ninth Fort.

"BRANDS PLUCKED FROM THE FIRE." Children who survived the war in hiding with Gentile families. The survivors of the Kovno ghetto gathered up these children and restored them to the Jewish community.